THE LITTLE BOOK OF
FRAUDS

DAVID OWEN

THE LITTLE BOOK OF
FRAUDS

From Enron to Madoff, 50 economic
and political scandals that
shocked the world

DAVID OWEN

METRO BOOKS

NEW YORK

Contents

6   Introduction

8   Part One: Financial fraud
The South Sea Bubble 1720 · The Yazoo Land Fraud 1796
· Napoleon Death Fraud 1814 · The Oregon Land Fraud 1870
· The Men Who Broke the Bank of England 1872 · The Original
Ponzi Scheme 1920 · Bottomly's Victory Bonds 1922 · The
Perfect Forgeries 1925 · The Vatican Bank Fraud 1982
· The Bank of Japan Scandal 1998 · Swiss Banks and the
Holocaust 2000 · The Enron Deception 2001 · The Pillar of
Wall Street 2008 · Satyam: Indian's 2008 · Stanford's
Billions 2009

48   Part Two: Corporate Fraud
The Crédit Mobilier Scandal 1872 · Lockheed Bribery
Scandals 1975 · The Recruit Scandal 1988 · Guinness
ShareScandal 1990 · WorldCom Bankruptcy Fraud 1992
· The Barings Bank Cover-up 1995 · The Air Canada Airbus
Affair 1995 · Robbing the Shareholders 2005 · The Chinese
Pensions Scandal 2006 · Jérome Kerviel and Société
Général 2008 · The Hong-Kong Share Fraud 2009

74   **Part Three: Cover-ups and Deceptions**
Watergate 1974 · Rainbow Warrior 1985 · The Iran-Contra
Scandal 1986 · The Marcos Dictatorship 1986 · Disaster
at Chernobyl 1986 · Maxwell and the Missing Pensions
1991 · The Australian Wheat Board 2006 · The Litvinenko
Murder 2006

94   **Part Four: Political Scandals**
Teapot Dome 1922 · Cash for Honours 1922 · The Profumo
Affair 1963 · The Chappaquiddick Incident 1969 · Willy
Brandt's Spy Secretary 1974 · Cash for Questions 1994
· Impeach the President 1998 · The Berlusconi Years 2009
· MPs Expenses scandal 2009

118   **Part Five: Military Scandals**
L'Affaire Dreyfus 1894 · The Tonkin Gulf Incident
1964 · Massacre at My Lai 1968 · Operation Menu 1969
· Weapons of Mass Destruction 2003 · Use of Torture
2005 · Extraordinary Rendition 2006

139   Glossary
141   Sources
142   Index

Introduction

Frauds and scandals have an enduring fascination for various reasons. Sometimes we suspect a meteoric rise to fame and fortune hides a shady secret to explain such spectacular progress. Did those involved cash in on family relationships, underworld connections, or bribing the right people who could influence things in their favor? If some or all of those factors were present, then we can be consoled in two ways. Either we feel excused for our lack of success by retaining the moral high ground, or we can comfort ourselves that had we too been able to exploit these hidden factors, maybe we could have had the rewards our ingenuity and hard work deserve.

What about those cases where more direct criminal activities are concerned? Then the eventual downfall of those responsible becomes a reassurance that perhaps Providence, like Justice, is blind, and the workings of chance are fairer than they sometimes seem. Sometimes an investment scheme is so dramatically successful that those signing up have fortunes made for them with little effort on their parts. Of course the crashing back to earth that follows the collapse of a pyramid scam or a manipulation of the market can be truly tragic for those indirectly involved. Yet for the rest of us, they provide a welcome condemnation of a system seeming only to reward the unworthy.

For politicians having to tread an ever more perilous path between the deals and compromises needed to place them on the route to power and the deepening scrutiny and cynicism of the electorate, life grows ever more difficult. In some cases, those caught out covering up past mistakes can earn our sympathy. In others, we can feel justifiably angry at the breathtaking arrogance which brings them down in the first place. And wherever innocent people have suffered because of lies and cover-ups by those higher up the power structure, we can genuinely enjoy reading of justice being done or reputations being restored where no blame should have existed in the first place.

These are some of the reasons why the cases outlined in this book carry a message for all of us. Where people have been robbed, discredited, exploited, or misled, then punishing those responsible either financially or by the loss of reputation or liberty can help redress the balance. But there remains one area which should sound a note of concern for all of us. In so many cases included in the book, a deception could only be created in the first place because people wanted to believe what seemed to be on offer. Huge increases in the value of our savings, or the profits of the companies or institutions for which we work, and the resulting rise in our own standing within those organizations, are highly desirable outcomes. Too desirable, perhaps, for us to subject those who try to sell us these outcomes, to the searching scrutiny needed. In the end, believing is far easier than checking. And if we suffer the inevitable losses and disappointments, then some of the blame must rest with us, as well as with those who deceived us. A final reason for reading this book is to enable us to reflect that "there but for the grace of God go I," and to make a firm resolution not to make those same errors of judgment ourselves.

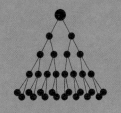

Part One:
Financial Fraud

The South Sea Bubble (1720)

A plan to fund the 18th-century British National Debt and repay the costs of war with Spain by trading with her South American colonies created a huge investment bubble, sending share prices sky-high, then ruining thousands when they inevitably fell.

Background

The early 1700s saw investment famine in Britain. Enterprises like the East India Company paid massive returns, but shares were scarce and difficult to come by. In 1711 the British Government gave the newly-formed South Sea Company a monopoly in trade with Spanish possessions in South America. In return the government received a £10 million loan to cover the costs of the War of the Spanish Succession. Investors flocked to take part in a fresh opportunity.

Deception

The resulting South Sea Bubble was a massive self-deception. Like the huge rise in tulip prices on the Dutch stock market a century before, none of the eager speculators paused to consider the true value of what was being traded. As new shares were issued and prices rose, a whole series of other companies appeared to offer even more fanciful opportunities. The Mississippi Company planned to refinance by replacing gold and silver in the financial system with paper money, soon they were worth more than the entire economy of France. Others were formed to buy bogland in Ireland, to reclaim sunshine from vegetables and even one for a mysterious objective which was never revealed, from which the promoter fled after collecting £2,000 from investors.

Above *The Bubblers Medley, or a Sketch of the Times: Being Europes Memorial for the year 1720.* This satirical print includes poems, images, playing cards, and newspaper clippings that all focus on the South Sea Bubble scandal.

The South Sea Company planned to make money from South American trade and by buying more and more government debt at favorable interest rates. When relations between Spain and Britain worsened in 1718, the directors spent heavily on bribing politicians, talking up the value of the shares, and convincing more investors that a long-term future was assured. The share price climbed from £128 in January 1720 to £550 in May, and by early August had reached £1,000 per share.

Exposure

At this point the directors realized trade with Spanish America was extremely disappointing. The Spanish would only allow the company to use one single ship carrying 500 tons of cargo and their high duty on slaves made even this part of the business unprofitable. When some sold their shareholdings in secrecy, the news leaked and prices began to tumble. Within a month shares had fallen back to £150 and by the end of the year to £100. Banks, merchants, and investors faced bankruptcy and the whole financial system was on the brink of collapsing.

Fallout

Parliament's investigation blamed politicians and the company directors. John Aislabie, the Chancellor of the Exchequer—the British Government's senior finance minister—was jailed for fraud and the Postmaster General, James Craggs the Elder, was impeached and died in disgrace. The company directors had their estates seized and sold to help meet investors' losses. Robert Walpole, the new First Lord of the Treasury—effectively Prime Minister—took strong action to prevent panic spreading. The company's stock was split between the East India Company and the Bank of England, ironically the South Sea Company continued operating for more than a century as an aid to help manage the National Debt.

The Yazoo Land Fraud (1796)

Huge demand for land in newly independent America created ample opportunity for large-scale scandals.

Background

Following independence, the US was expanding rapidly, and states were making large land claims beyond their western frontiers. In Georgia, these were known as "Yazoo lands" after the river that flowed through the area. The state was too weak to defend these claims and they were happy to sell off the land to speculators willing to settle on it, huge areas were sold off at rock-bottom prices. The state governor, George Matthews, passed the Yazoo Act on January 7, 1795, selling off 35 million acres of territory to four companies for a total price of $500,000.

Deception

On the face of it, this was perfectly legal. But the methods used by supporters of the Act to ensure it was passed were scandalous. These supporters stood to make huge fortunes from what was an enormous giveaway of public assets. The leader of this group, Senator James Gunn, had used gifts of land and cash in a shameless bribery campaign directed at lawmakers, newspaper owners and editors, politicians, and other people with influence in Georgian society, all backed up with threats and coercion against potential opponents.

Exposure

When opponents found that a much higher bid of $800,000 for the land, from the Georgia Union Company, including a $40,000 cash advance deposit, had been totally ignored, rising public anger triggered a campaign to overturn the act. Georgia's leading Republican senator, James Jackson, resigned his office to run a cleverly planned operation aimed at mobilizing local support through the press and local grand jury hearings charged with hearing individual corruption cases. In 1796, he and his supporters drew up the Rescinding Act, which was signed into law by then Governor, Jared Irwin. This overturned the Yazoo deals. Records relating to the land sales were destroyed, and public anger ensured that anyone who had played a part in the corruption were effectively barred from public office.

Fallout

There remained the question of what to do with the Yazoo lands. Georgia had the option of yielding its rights over the territory to the US Congress, but Jackson was worried that a sympathetic vote by the Federalist majority in Congress would cancel their reforms and the land would be handed back to those involved in the scandal. They therefore postponed action until 1802, when the Republicans regained a majority in Congress, and the Yazoo lands were handed over. This was followed by a series of lawsuits from those who had bought parcels of land. Finally, the US Chief Justice ruled the Rescinding Act had technically violated the constitutional law of contract. Four years later, the US Congress solved the problem by repaying the claimants from a $5 million fund created from the proceeds of legitimate land sales in the neighboring Mississippi Territory.

Above Map of the areas of land granted to the companies involved in the Yazoo Land Fraud.

Napoleon Death Fraud (1814)

In days of slower communications, the rumor of a potentially world-shaking event could trigger a surge in share values, allowing those "in the know" to make a fortune.

Background

By February 1814, England had been fighting France for almost a decade. With the Emperor Napoleon facing defeat, the London Stock Exchange would see a share boom once peace was declared. Moreover, those who reacted fastest would see the greatest gains.

Deception

The eagerly awaited news arrived on the morning of Monday, February 21, when an officer claiming to be the Colonel du Bourg, *aide de camp* to Viscount Cathcart, a general in the Allied Army of Liberation, visited the Ship Inn at Dover, UK. He announced that Napoleon had been killed, and the Bourbons were once more on the throne of France. He asked that the news be sent immediately to the Admiralty in London using the chain of semaphore stations linking the port to the capital. He set off on horseback to relay the news at each inn he passed on his way. He was followed by a coach carrying three men in French officers' uniforms, passing out leaflets celebrating the Bourbon restoration and the Allied victory. The Stock Exchange reacted quickly, and the price of government securities soared at the first message, fell back slightly until the coach arrived with the second message, and then rallied again. By the afternoon, the government refused to confirm the news, and prices sank back to their original levels. When it became clear Napoleon was still alive, it was obvious that a fraud had been committed.

Exposure

The Stock Exchange launched an investigation, and found that £1.1 million worth of government stocks had been sold during the period when prices were high, having only been bought the week before at their original level. The "French Officers" had disappeared without a trace but the individual posing as Colonel du Bourg was later identified as a penniless soldier of fortune named Random de Berenger. Among those who had benefited from the surge in share prices were one of Britain's foremost naval heroes, Captain Lord Cochrane, his uncle, and his financial advisor. All three were charged with fraud, found guilty, fined, and imprisoned after being placed in the pillory—a restraint for the neck and wrists which prevented the victim from dodging rotten vegetables and other garbage thrown by the crowds attending the punishment. In Lord Cochrane's case, he was also dismissed from the Navy and expelled from the Order of the Bath.

Fallout

On the face of it, this was a clear and simple attempt to manipulate the market for personal gain. But Cochrane had been an uncompromising opponent of incompetence both within the Navy and of corruption in public life in general, and had made many powerful enemies. He insisted on maintaining his innocence, and claimed that the treatment of his case by the presiding judge, Lord Ellenborough, had been biased and unjust. Much public opinion supported him, and he was immediately reelected to Parliament following his release. He left Britain to take a leading part in the independence struggle of Greece and the new South American republics of Chile and Brazil. Finally, in 1832 he was given a Royal Pardon and allowed to rejoin the Navy with the rank of Rear Admiral. He died in 1860 with all his honors restored to him.

The Oregon Land Fraud (1870)

As the US rail network grew, every new line caused land along the route to soar in value, providing fraudsters with huge opportunities.

Background

In 1870, the Oregon and California Railroad was given the right to build a southbound route from Portland, Oregon to California. With it went a total of three million acres of land along the route, enough to be sold as small 160 acre plots at the bargain price of $400 apiece. This low price was used to encourage people to settle in the area.

Deception

Unfortunately, the land itself was of little commercial value, apart from the huge forests it contained. A railroad official named Ned Harriman decided that there was money to be made from selling the land in larger packets to companies able to harvest timber. Railroad companies were required by law to sell land to individuals. To get around this, Harriman recruited an accomplice, one Stephen A. Douglas Puter, to tour the dockside bars in Portland and persuade drifters to come to the land office and register with the rail company as potential settlers. They would then sign away their land rights to the conspirators, who would group the holdings into larger areas to be auctioned off to timber companies.

Exposure

All went well until Harriman and Puter fell into dispute, and Puter was dismissed. An accountant working for one of the timber companies became aware of the deception, he realized Harriman was boosting the prices the companies had to pay for forest land. He told a reporter on the local paper, *The Oregonian*. When all was exposed, in Puter testified against his former collaborator and the scandal was totally revealed.

Fallout

The shockwaves spread far and wide. Harriman and Puter may have been responsible for running the fraud, but the people who were to benefit from their ingenuity included US Senator John H. Mitchell and two members of the House of Representatives, Binger Hermann and John N. Williamson. In all, more than a thousand cases were brought, though these were soon reduced to the 35 most serious offenders. These included Senator Mitchell—found guilty of using his privileged position to help clients make fradulent land claims—he was sentenced to six months jail and a $1,000 fine. Before he could mount an appeal, he died from the after effects of having a tooth extracted.

John N. Williamson was accused of trying to make illegal land claims, but was acquitted in 1908 by the US Supreme Court because of reports of jury tampering and threatening of witnesses. Binger Hermann was found not guilty on charges of destroying public documents to cover his tracks, and his trial for involvement in the land fraud resulted in a deadlocked jury. One other prominent defendant, Oregon's District Attorney John Hicklin Hall, whose lax prosecution of the case resulted in President Theodore Roosevelt dismissing him in 1905 and replacing him with Francis J. Heney, the man who prosecuted him. Hall was convicted in 1908 for failing to prosecute the land companies involved and of using inside knowledge for his own advantage. He too, escaped justice, when he was later pardoned by President Taft.

The Men Who Broke the Bank of England (1872)

Astute businessmen from Chicago spotted a weakness in the Bank of England's security system, and defrauded it of £500,000.

Background

Defrauding the Bank of England should have been an impossible target for even the most accomplished of criminals. Yet George and Austin Bidwell, brothers from Chicago, who had carried out frauds all over the world, finally stumbled across a gap in the bank's security which presented them with a stupendous opportunity.

Deception

It appeared that the Bank of England trusted its customers in two surprising respects: it asked for no references and it allowed them to draw large amounts of cash against bills presented by responsible institutions without checking their reliability or returning the documents for verification. This allowed the Bidwells to pose as immensely wealthy cotton brokers from the US and open a series of London bank accounts. They moved their own limited funds backwards and forwards to create an impression of enormous financial resources. Finally, in 1855, they chose a smaller branch of the Bank, which had been opened in Burlington Street in London's West End. The plausible George Bidwell soon befriended Colonel Francis, the branch manager, and the brothers managed to find several examples of genuine bills of exchange from major banks, like Rothschilds, which they were able to forge with great accuracy. They presented these at the branch, signed by Austin Bidwell as "F.A.Warren" and withdrew a total of £500,000, in cash, with no problems at all.

Exposure

All went well until a tiny mistake revealed everything. Austin Bidwell forgot to date one of the forged bills he had signed before leaving on his honeymoon. The Bank returned it to the institution which had issued it, who insisted it was a forgery. The Bidwells escaped with the police on their heels. Austin eventually went into hiding in Havana, Cuba, there he was identified by a British detective a year later and was arrested. After a long fight against extradition, he was finally sent back to England to await trial with his brother who had been arrested in Edinburgh, Scotland.

Fallout

Most of the money had been traced and recovered by the time the brothers went on trial. Both were found guilty and sentenced to life imprisonment with hard labor. Under the harsh conditions, their health broke down and George was released on compassionate grounds in 1887. After a vigorous campaign led by their sister Mrs. Henrietta Mott, Austin was also released in 1892. He died in Butte, Montana seven years later. At the time, he and George were said to have arrived in town with funds from East Coast backers to set up a mining operation, which was almost certainly an attempt at yet another fraud.

The Original Ponzi Scheme (1920)

Carlo Ponzi developed an ingenious fraud which depended on using existing investors' funds to attract new victims to his apparently successful scheme.

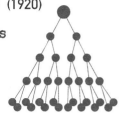

Background

Carlo Pietro Giovanni Guglielmo Tebaldo Ponzi was born in Italy in 1882. He arrived in Boston, Massachusetts in November 1903, but moved to Montreal, Canada in 1907 to work in Luigi Zarossi's highly successful Italian bank. Appointed manager in 1911, he realized Zarossi was using new deposits to keep the bank afloat. Zarossi soon fled to Mexico with the money, and Ponzi was jailed for three years for forging a check to fund his return to the US.

Deception

After two more years in an American jail for smuggling illegal Italian immigrants across the border, he returned to Boston and started a string of failed business ventures. One was a business catalog, which brought a letter from a Spanish company, enclosing an International Reply Coupon (IRC). Ponzi realized IRCs could be exchanged for stamps wherever it was sent, and in the financial turmoil following the First World War, IRCs bought in Italy would be worth far more when exchanged for stamps in the US. His plan to exploit this was legal, but turned sour when he began borrowing money from investors. As more money was raised, he paid back initial investors from new deposits coming in, and for the time being, all was well. He paid salesmen huge commissions to recruit more savers. By the summer of 1920, he was banking $250,000 a day, equivalent to $2.75 million today. This was a classic pyramid-selling scam whereby existing investors could only be paid by money contributed from new investors, and was unsustainable over the long term.

Exposure

In July 1920, Ponzi bought a controlling interest in a Boston bank, the
Hanover Trust, and a luxurious mansion in Lexington. But his lavish lifestyle
was funded by new depositors flooding the scheme, rather than the IRC plan
he had started with. For the figures to add up, Ponzi's company would have
to buy 160 million IRCs, but only some 27,000 were circulating at the time.

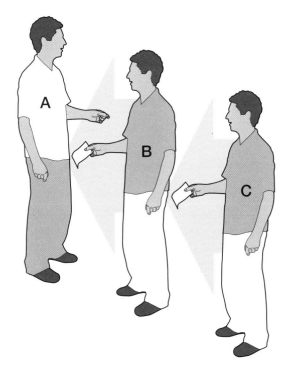

Above A diagram showing how a Ponzi scheme works. The fraudster (A) entices his first
victim (B) into his "lucrative" scheme by offering amazing returns on his investments. In fact,
in order to pay B the promised returns, the fraudster takes the money of another victim (C)
and pays B. The cycle will continue as long as there are other victims that pay into the scheme.

Even if they had bought sufficient IRCs, the costs of buying and redeeming each low-value certificate could never generate a profit. When a Boston financial journalist suggested there was no honest way Ponzi could return 50 percent on investments after just six weeks, Ponzi sued for libel and won $500,000 damages. When the *Boston Post* praised his scheme on July 20, 1920, the threat seemed over, but the paper's own reporters were digging for information. Then, on that same day, Ponzi was questioned by Massachusetts officials. Six days later, the *Boston Post* published the first in a series of much more critical articles. They commissioned financial expert, Clarence Barron, to check Ponzi's claims.

Within days, depositors queued to get their money back—Ponzi served them coffee and doughnuts, and promised all was well, but cracks were spreading. On August 2, the paper declared he was some $4.5 million in debt. A week later, the Massachusetts authorities found the truth was even worse: He was $7 million in debt. They froze his bank's accounts.

Fallout

On August 11, the *Boston Post* revealed Ponzi's past in Canada and he was arrested on the first of a series of fraud charges. His bank collapsed, followed by five others, and most investors lost their life savings. The *Boston Post* won a Pulitzer Prize for exposing the fraud and Ponzi was given a three and a half year jail sentence for Federal fraud convictions. He was then rearrested on 22 more Massachusetts state charges and given another seven years. He was bailed in September 1925 pending an appeal and was found selling tracts of flooded swampland in Florida, promising investors to double their money within a month. Still an Italian citizen, he was recommended for deportation after serving his sentence. In Italy, he worked for the dictator Mussolini before emigrating to South America where he died in destitution in 1949, finally admitting his guilt after years of claiming innocence.

Bottomley's Victory Bonds (1922)

Horatio Bottomley became a middleman selling shares in the British Government's expensive Victory Bonds to less well-heeled investors, but failed to pay them the promised interest.

Background

Horatio Bottomley was born to a poor family in London in 1860. Apprenticed to a law firm where one partner defrauded clients by inflating their bills, Bottomley soon became a successful businessman and publisher, and was elected to Parliament, though he lost his seat due to bankruptcy in 1912. In December 1918 he was reelected Liberal Member of Parliament for South Hackney. In the following summer the government faced the task of paying off the huge costs of four years of world war. They introduced Victory Bonds at £5 a piece; this was twice the average weekly wage. Bottomley saw this as a major opportunity.

Deception

He announced that anyone who sent him a pound would have a one-fifth share in a Victory Bond which would be entered into a prize draw for the interest earned by the bonds. He was totally unprepared for the resulting public enthusiasm. Donations came in at the rate of £100,000 a day, while Bottomley waited for the bond price to drop before actually buying any, his dozen inexperienced clerks were overwhelmed by the paperwork, and there were long delays in sending out share certificates to eager applicants. As delays lengthened, the public mood changed and people began demanding their money back.

Exposure

By the end of 1919, Bottomley had spent £500,000 to buy bonds at bargain prices, but had already had to refund 150,000 subscribers. The funds needed to make repayments to other subscribers were vanishing fast, some stolen by his own clerks, but others by Bottomley himself, used to buy control of newspapers or settle his huge gambling debts. Pamphlets appeared claiming he was defrauding people of their savings, but Bottomley developed an ingenious defence. He would pay an agent, Reuben Bigland, to produce similar pamphlets and then win a libel action, so making it legally impossible for anyone to repeat the accusations. The decisive blow fell when Bottomley had a dispute with Bigland, the printer of his fake pamphlets. Bigland began printing new tell-all pamphlets, which, with his inside knowledge, proved fatal. Rival newspapers took up the accusations, and Bottomley was charged with fraud in May 1922.

Fallout

Bottomley defended himself, but the judge sentenced him to seven years in jail. He was expelled from the House of Commons for a second time, and entered prison at the age of sixty, overweight, and a heavy drinker. He was eventually released in 1927, in poor health. He tried to start another magazine, named *John Blunt* to try and cash in on the earlier success of his magazine *John Bull*. He wrote articles about his prison experiences, but the magazine failed and the commissions dried up. He was finally reduced to appearances in music halls, telling audiences about his colorful life. In late 1932 he suffered a heart attack on stage at the Windmill Theatre, he recovered to give a final interview to the *Daily Mail* in 1933. He died on May 26, virtually penniless.

The Perfect Forgeries (1925)

Counterfeiters face an almost
impossible task in producing
convincing copies of banknotes.
Instead of counterfeiting,
Arthur Virgilio Alves Reis
forged the paperwork to order
genuine notes instead.

Background

Arthur Virgilio Reis worked for Portugal's colonial service, and knew that
counterfeiting Portuguese banknotes would be impossible. However, in
1924, he found that some Bank of Portugal notes were printed by Waterlow
in England. He devised a plan to place a fake order for banknotes from
Waterlow for Portugal's African colony of Angola.

Deception

He recruited three accomplices, originally as innocent colleages: Dutch
businessman, Karel Marang, who had diplomatic status as Persian Consul-
General at the Hague; a German businessman, Gustav Hennies; and José
Bandeira, brother of the Portuguese Minister at the Hague. Reis showed them
a forged letter, apparently signed by the Portuguese Finance Minister and the
High Commissioner for Angola, giving him authority to arrange a £1 million
loan for the colony, to be paid by a special printing of a quarter million 500-
escudo notes. Marang went to England to show the document to Waterlow's,
with a letter of introduction from Bandeira's brother. The printers wanted
written confirmation from the Governor of the Bank of Portugal and Marang
confirmed this would be sent immediately.

Reis forged an official letter and contracts for the special printing. The
letter explained the notes would only circulate in Angola, so to save time the

printers could use the plates and serial numbers of an earlier issue. The new notes would be overprinted "Angola' on arrival, and Marang, would carry the notes in four consignments in the diplomatic bag. With such convincing paperwork, the order went smoothly, and the notes reached Lisbon safely. There Reis had opened his own bank, the Bank of Angola and Metropole, to exchange the cash for foreign banknotes and company shares. Within three months of the final consignment—July 1925—he and his fellow conspirators were preparing documents to order a second consignment, twice the size of the first.

Exposure

In December 1925, a cashier at another bank noticed that some apparently genuine 500 escudo notes had the same serial numbers as those already in circulation. When inspectors raided the Oporto branch of Reis's bank, they found bundles of perfect new notes, all with the serial numbers of existing banknotes. Reis was arrested, but produced forged letters showing he was the innocent victim of a plot devised by the Governor and directors of the Bank of Portugal, who were arrested as well. Eventually they were able to prove their innocence. Waterlow, too, came under suspicion, but they were able to show they had been duped.

Fallout

Finally, in May 1930, Reis was put on trial and pleaded guilty, he was given a twenty-year sentence, together with Bandeira. At the time of their crime, the maximum sentence was three years in prison, but the government introduced retrospective legislation to increase this to a maximum of 25 years. Hennies fled justice by escaping to Germany, where he died six years later. Marang tried in his native Holland and was jailed for 11 months for receiving stolen property. Reis was eventually released in 1945 and died ten years later with nothing to show for his ingenious forgery scheme.

The Vatican Bank Fraud (1982)

The Catholic Banco Ambrosiano
became involved in several
murders, the disappearance
of 1.4 billion dollars, and
alleged complicity in the
death of a Pope.

Background

In 1975, Roberto Calvi was appointed chairman of Banco Ambrosiano. He
created offshore banking companies in South America and the Caribbean
and bought into other Italian banks. His bank backed the *Corriere della Sera*
newspaper and provided funds for both Italian and overseas political parties.

Deception

Calvi used his offshore companies to move money out of Italy against foreign
exchange restrictions and also manipulated share prices to make massive
profits on insider trading—buying low-price shares knowing their value was
about to soar. He also underwrote huge unsecured loans. Two years after his
appointment, a Bank of Italy report predicted that Banco Ambrosiano was
heading for financial disaster, and that criminal charges were pending. But
these were violent times in Italy and the investigating magistrate dealing with
the case, Emilio Alessandrini, was murdered by a left-wing group, while the
Bank of Italy official who produced the report, Marcio Sarcinelli, was jailed
on charges later revealed as false.

Exposure

In 1981, Italian police raided the headquarters of a secretive Masonic lodge—
P2 or Propaganda Du—searching for evidence that its Master, Licio Gelli,
was conspiring to overthrow the government. They also found evidence that

Roberto Calvi had illegally exported $26 million to Switzerland. He was found guilty and sentenced to four years in prison, but was released pending an appeal. The Bank of Italy auditors found that $1.4 billion was missing from Banco Ambrosiano accounts and that this money had been loaned to questionable companies in Panama apparently controlled by Calvi. He immediately fled to London on a forged passport. On June 17, 1982 Calvi's private secretary, Graziella Corrocher, jumped through a fourth-floor window at the bank's headquarters to her death, leaving a note which said Calvi should be twice cursed for the damage he caused to the bank and its employees. On the following day, Calvi's corpse was found hanging beneath London's Blackfriars Bridge, his suit pockets filled with stones and banknotes. Forensic evidence showed this was no suicide—he had almost certainly been killed elsewhere and his body moved to the bridge, which had symbolic links to the P2 Masonic Lodge, whose members were known as "friars" and habitually wore black.

Above Roberto Calvi, chairman of the Banco Ambrosiano, arrives at trial. Milan, May 29, 1981.

Fallout

Payments to Calvi's offshore companies were cut off, causing their collapse. Banco Ambrosiano was reconstituted as the Nuovo Banco Ambrosiano, and the Vatican itself paid $250 billion to meet part of the costs of the illegal loans. Archbishop Paul Marcinkus, the American-born head of the Vatican's own bank, served on the board of Calvi's overseas subsidiary, and was alleged to have boosted the credibility of Calvi's Panamanian companies by signing letters that they were controlled by the Vatican Bank. In return, his own position was protected by Calvi's signed denials that the Vatican Bank had any role in the transaction at all. When questioned by Bank of Italy officials, Marcinkus insisted he had only done what Calvi had asked and refused to answer further questions. Attempts to extradite him from Vatican territory failed, and he died in America in 2006, in relative obscurity.

Not everyone concerned was so fortunate. Michele Sindona, an Italian-American financier sold two companies to Calvi and his bank for a greatly inflated $100 million in 1973. When Sindona was made bankrupt six years later, the liquidator of his companies, Giorgio Ambrosoli, revealed a $5.6 million commission had been paid to an American bishop and a Milanese banker, later confirmed as Marcinkus and Calvi. Soon afterwards Ambrosoli was killed outside his home by three gunmen. Sindona himself first alerted the authorities to Calvi's crimes, but was jailed for instigating Ambrosoli's murder, and died in prison in 1986 after drinking a cup of coffee that had been laced with cyanide. And allegations persist that Pope John Paul I, who only held the office for 33 days, was poisoned on September 28, 1978 after announcing he would investigate the Vatican's involvement in the banking scandal.

The Bank of Japan scandal (1998)

Many financial scandals involve the misuse or loss of investors' money and the ruin of lives, but Japan's greatest banking scandal involved the sale of information in return for rewards as prosaic as lavish meals and entertainment.

Background

People working for the largest and most powerful banks have access to enormously valuable insider information, which less fortunate organizations would give a great deal to learn. Consequently, bribery is always a possibility, because the potential returns from insider knowledge are far more than the amounts involved in persuading people to release the information.

Deception

Japan's largest and most prestigious financial institution, the Bank of Japan, was the center of the country's greatest financial scandal. Yasuzuki Yoshizawa, head of the Bank's capital markets division was a natural target for bribery from smaller and less powerful banks wanting to buy information. Over a four-year period beginning in May 1993, he accepted bribes totaling between 4 million and 7 million yen from the Industrial Bank of Japan and the Sanwa Bank. This was merely a small part of a whole culture of payments and kickbacks involving bank employees. The system was so widespread that it even developed its own slang terms—for example, if a bank bribed someone with a dinner costing 20,000 yen, this was referred to as a "splash," if the amount paid for the meal was more than 100,000 yen, it qualified as a "plunge."

Exposure

Uncovering the scandal was the result of official government suspicions that bank employees were trying to bribe civil servants to persuade them to leak sensitive information. When investigators traced two officials who had suspiciously close links to major banks, their widening search eventually implicated Yoshizawa, and the whole network was exposed. Though no actual laws had been broken, it was clear that sensitive information was traded in return for lavish entertainment, often with the connivance of Mr. Yoshizawa. Though bank officials claimed they had never set out to persuade financial firms to pay them in cash or gifts in kind, by providing lavish meals or offering discounts on highly sought-after golf club memberships—extremely expensive in Japan—it was clear that most knew and accepted the system. Yoshizawa was fired, and the Governor of the Bank, Yasuo Matsushita, resigned because the scandal had emerged under his responsibility, though without his knowledge. Three of his advisors and two executive directors of the bank were punished with a 20 percent pay cut for between one and five months. In addition, his newly appointed replacement, Masaru Hiyami, and four other executive directors accepted a voluntary cut of one fifth of one month's salary to show their determination to restore the bank's credibility. They also instigated an investigation of all 600 senior management employees, to determine the nature of their contacts with outside banks and organizations to decide whether any had contravened the law.

Fallout

The investigation took two months, and uncovered an astonishingly widespread culture of favors and kickbacks for valuable inside information. As a result of its disclosures, 98 Bank of Japan staff were disciplined by written and verbal warnings, and in some cases by large salary cuts. Other banks involved, including the Industrial Bank of Japan, the Asahi Bank, the Sanwa Bank, and the Sumitomo Bank, all took similar action on the pay of their chairmen, presidents, and senior officials. New regulations were put in place to guard against any further sales of sensitive information to third parties in return for bribes or gifts in kind.

Swiss Banks and the Holocaust (2000)

Swiss Banks built their reputation
on the secrecy they maintained
over investors' accounts,
which put them under massive
pressure when their accounts
held assets taken from victims
of Nazi oppression.

Background

After the end of the Second World War, investigations into the vast wealth confiscated from their victims by the Nazis led to the doors of the famously secretive Swiss banks, which remained resolutely closed to survivors and family members alike.

Deception

In many cases, information was only available to those who had originally opened the accounts: either officials in the Nazi regime, or those who had become victims of that regime after placing their savings in the safety of the Swiss banks. In most of these cases, the original account holders had vanished into the concentration camps and their surviving relatives were powerless to make claims as inheritors of the property. The banks insisted on formal death certificates before taking action, and because these did not exist, they were able to continue holding onto the assets.

Exposure

With more and more claims being refused by the Swiss banks for lack of documentation, suspicions grew that this was a deliberate obstruction. In 1974, the banks admitted they had found a total of 4.68 million Swiss francs in dormant accounts, which they had already voluntarily transferred to Swiss charities and the governments of Poland and Hungary. Opponents claimed this was merely a tiny fraction of the disputed assets, and as frustration grew, many Holocaust survivors and their relatives—principally in the US—mounted a determined legal challenge to recover their property. Finally, in October 1996, the Swiss ambassador to the US, Carlo Jagmetti, admitted that some banks had obstructed attempts to have funds released. Three months later Christoph Meili, a security guard at the Union Bank of Switzerland, acted to prevent the bank destroying wartime records. Meili was fired for his pains, and received death threats, which led to him being the first Swiss citizen ever to be granted political asylum in the US.

On January 29, 1997, the city of New York announced it was considering an official boycott of Swiss banks in protest at their refusal to cooperate. On February 6, three Swiss banks announced they would set up a joint fund of $70 million to meet all outstanding claims, while still insisting that the disputed accounts contained a tiny fraction of the amounts being claimed. In 1999, an international panel of historians claimed there was evidence that the Swiss National Bank had continued to accept substantial gold deposits even after these had been shown to have been stolen from individual victims or the treasuries of conquered countries.

Fallout

In 2001 the tribunal charged with tracing ownership of dormant accounts found that only 200 out of a total of 5,570 accounts checked actually belonged to Holocaust victims, containing a total of some $12 million. The remainder mostly belonged to non-Jewish clients with no link to the Holocaust, and half the accounts checked contained less than 1,000 Swiss francs apiece. This contrasts with the claim by Paul Volcker, former head of the US Federal Reserve Board who oversaw a joint US-Swiss bank audit, that some 54,000 accounts were opened by Holocaust victims during the Nazi oppression, with deposits totaling between $700 million and $1.3 billion.

Nevertheless, the banks have been making larger repayments in the face of increasing legal pressure. In 2000, the threat of massive US class action lawsuits pressured the Credit Suisse and Union Bank of Switzerland to release

Above Rabbi Marvin Hier, founder of the Nazi-hunting Simon Wiesenthal Center, holds a list of Nazi officials and Second World War German business men who may have transferred Holocaust victims looted assets.

$1.25 billion for outstanding claims, and in November 2000 it was agreed that $800 million of this fund would be used to meet specific and convincing claims relating to individual accounts, with the remainder being distributed to former refugees and slave laborers who had suffered at Nazi hands. As repayments proceeded over recent years, the banks have at last began to lift their curtain of secrecy and release more vital information about the holders and contents of the disputed accounts.

The Enron Deception (2001)

The collapse of the energy giant, Enron Corporation, in 2001 was the largest American corporate bankruptcy at the time, and with it went the company's auditors, Arthur Andersen, then one of the five largest accountancy firms worldwide.

Background

Enron was formed in 1985 by the merger of two natural gas pipeline operators, and by 1992, US deregulation of the natural gas market had made the company the biggest natural gas supplier in North America. By 2001 the company's wealth enabled it to diversify into water and electricity supply, paper and pulp production, and financial services. For most of this period, its share value climbed along with other major companies, but from 1999 onwards its book value soared to new heights and its continued success seemed assured.

Deception

In spite of its apparently huge resources, Enron was becoming known for the lack of detailed information in its financial statements and the complexity of some of its dealings. This was all made worse by accounting techniques allowed at the time. In the company's earlier days, its costs and income had related to the realities of supplying the natural gas which was its core business on a real-time basis. But by 2000, it was setting up deals to create future income and using estimates of projected profits as if these were guaranteed. In addition, many of its operations were being switched to other companies referred to as "special purpose entities." These were being presented as independent companies by bending the rules on how independence was defined in accounting terms, and this allowed Enron to inflate its value and income while reducing its apparent liabilities. The company's accounts were audited by the accountancy firm, Arthur Andersen. They were being paid enormous sums for the service which created a potential conflict of interest—it was unlikely Arthur Andersen would criticize such a major client. All this was causing more and more unease within the business community.

Exposure

By the summer of 2001, Enron's steady growth had begun to falter. Though the company reported a tripling of earnings, profits had remained static and the share price had fallen more than 30 percent in a year from its $90 high. Problems were mounting in areas like its broadband services and the building

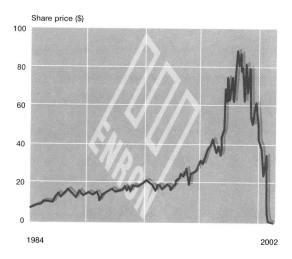

Above A graph showing the rapid decline in value of Enron shares after the uncovering of one of the largest business frauds of all time.

of a large power station in India. Finally, the company's newly appointed chief executive, Jeffrey Skilling, resigned after just six months in the job, having sold 450,000 shares in the company before he left. Chairman Kenneth Lay took over, but shares continued to slide. Ironically, the complexity of the accounts was preventing analysts from estimating the real value of the company. By October 2001 the company was planning to sell off parts of the business but, following an announcement that the US Securities and Exchange Commission was to investigate some of its dealings, shares were now worth a quarter of their previous peak. By November the company was looking for buyers as its credit rating fell and shares were now worth a mere $7 apiece. More information was coming to light on its accounting cover-ups, with the revelation that its earnings over the three years from 1997 had been overstated by almost $600 million. By November 19 the company revealed it could not meet its next debt repayments, and at the end of the month Enron filed for bankruptcy.

Fallout

With the failure of the company, 15,000 employees lost their jobs, their pensions, and most of their savings that had been invested in company schemes. The share value had collapsed back to ten cents, and liabilities amounted to some $23 billion. Since then, company bosses have been tried for offenses ranging from bank and security frauds to money laundering, conspiracy, insider trading, and making false statements to banks and auditors. Kenneth Lay died in July 2006, while awaiting sentence on six charges, while Skilling was sentenced to 24 years in prison on 19 of the 28 charges facing him. To prevent a recurrence of the catastrophe, tough new laws were introduced to make accounts more transparent and force companies to disclose more information on their financial operations.

The Pillar of Wall Street (2008)

Financier Bernard Madoff seemed
to make a fortune for his
investors, while committing the
largest investor fraud ever
committed by a single person.

Background

Bernard Madoff seemed to symbolize the classic American success story.
Born in 1938 from Eastern European immigrant stock, he worked as a
lifeguard and a sprinkler system installer until he used his $5,000 savings to
set up a penny-share trading company in his own name in 1960. His father-
in-law was a successful accountant who helped the Madoff business grow by
recommending his clients to use its services. It operated by handling orders
directly from retail brokers, and introduced a system where dealers paid
brokers for the right to carry out customers' orders. By making it difficult for
new investors to join what amounted to a restricted-membership club,
Madoff made his clients feel cherished and part of a uniquely successful
investment scheme, which offered consistently better-than-average returns.

Deception

Madoff cultivated close links with the financial world, serving at one time
as a non-executive chairman of the NASDAQ specialist stock market. He
was a board member of the industry's own regulatory group, the National
Association of Securities Dealers, and of the Securities Industry and Financial
Markets Association, and made huge donations to charities and political
funds. Perhaps because of this, he was able to operate for years without closer
scrutiny being paid to how he was able to offer investors such high returns
compared with his competitors. The truth was sadly familiar: like so many
operators of apparently highly successful investment schemes, when returns

began to fall, he switched to a Ponzi scheme (see page 21) or pyramid sales scam as far back as 1991. He began salting clients' investments away into his account with the Chase Manhattan Bank, and using this account to fund repayments to existing investors, until market conditions improved, hiding behind a screen of false accounting. Had his business continued to expand at an exponential rate, the deception might have been sustainable, but as expansion stalled, the money ran out all too quickly.

Exposure

Warnings were first sounded as early as 1999, when an expert financial analyst, Harry Markopolos studied Madoff's figures and reported him to the Security and Exchange Commission (SEC) that concluded it was mathematically impossible for him to have produced the returns he claimed, in existing market conditions. Others were suspicious that his increasingly complex business was monitored by a small three-person team, only one of whom was a qualified accountant. Five years later, when the SEC finally took a closer look, they concluded there were gaps and anomalies in the information Madoff had provided, but the following year

Above Bernard Madoff leaving the Federal Court after his bail hearing in New York, January 14, 2009.

the assistant director of the SEC's Office of Compliance, Inspections and Examinations married Madoff's niece Shana after the enquiry had been dropped.

When the final collapse of Madoff's operation came in early December 2008, his clients tried to withdraw funds as the markets declined. Madoff admitted to his sons that he was finding it all but impossible to pay some $7 billion due to clients, but he still intended to pay out $173 million in staff bonuses two months ahead of time. They questioned their father about the decision, whereupon he confessed that he had been running a Ponzi scheme and there was virtually nothing left in the company accounts. They contacted the Federal authorities, and Madoff was arrested and charged with fraud on December 11.

Fallout

The financial damage was catastrophic. Examination of the accounts showed that investors seemed to have been robbed of almost $65 billion, though some money had been paid to investors while the scam was still running. Former SEC chairman Harvey Pitt said the true losses to investors might be between $10 billion and $17 billion, and prosecutors estimated losses to accounts opened since 1999 totaled $13.2 billion. Madoff pleaded guilty to a total of 11 Federal charges including securities fraud, false accounting, perjury, and money laundering. On June 29, 2009, Madoff was sentenced to 150 years jail, without the possibility of parole.

Satyam: India's Enron (2008)

India's rapid emergence as a technological superpower has been hit by a billion dollar fraud scandal centered around one of its major companies.

Background

The rise of Satyam Computer Services (*satyam* is Sanskrit for "truth") to become India's fourth largest IT company represented one of the most brilliant success stories in the country's expanding technological economy. Founded in 1987 by B. Ramalinga Raju, it provided consultancy and IT services. All appeared to be going well, with business and profits booming, and more than 50,000 people on the payroll.

Deception

Behind Satyam's successful façade there was a widening gap between the company's accounts and the truth. Though the company had a range of blue-chip international clients and was quoted on the Indian National Stock Exchange as well as the Bombay Stock Exchange, both its assets and its cash reserves were grossly over-estimated and the gap with reality was widening. Finally, in December 2008, an apparently routine business decision led to the exposure of the country's greatest corporate financial scandal, which would come to be known as "India's Enron."

Exposure

On December 16, the company announced it would spend some $1.6 billion on the takeover of two companies, Maytas Property and Maytas Infra, both of which belonged to the two sons of Ramalinga Raju. Shareholders took fright and refused to accept the deal. Within seven hours they had halted the takeover

Above Employees of Indian software company Satyam shout supportive slogans in Hyderbad on January 8, 2009.

and the value of the company's shares began to plummet—losing more than 55 percent of their previous price on the New York Stock Exchange by the end of the day. A week later, the World Bank announced it was banning the company from dealing with its clients for eight years, for bribing Bank staff and not keeping accurate accounts, and its share price fell another 13 percent. The company scheduled a board meeting to carry out management reforms, but this was deferred to January 10, 2009. Three days before the meeting, chairman Ramalinga Raju resigned, admitting that he had been inflating profits and assets in a billion-dollar swindle. Indian police arrested Raju, his brother and managing director Rama Raju, and the company's chief financial officer on the day the meeting was due to be held. Investigators found that even the company's payroll records were inflated, with 13,000 of its claimed 53,000 employees entirely fictitious.

Fallout

The company's fall was spectacularly fast, as clients moved to protect their interests, US shareholders brought a series of lawsuits, and dealings in Satyam shares were suspended on the New York Stock Exchange. Reports spoke of 10,000 genuine staff possibly losing their jobs so the Indian Government replaced the company board with new directors to help keep it afloat. The role of PriceWaterhouseCoopers, the accountancy giant, as Satyam's auditors over ten years, was questioned, but the firm claimed that it could only audit the accounts which had been provided, and since these had been falsified, the audit was unreliable. To cope with the situation, strenuous attempts were made to produce a series of reliable accounts.

Finally, in March 2009, with Satyam shares in New York valued at only 6 percent of their 2008 peak, the new Satyam management invited takeover bids to rescue the company. In June it was bought by Tech Mahindra, another of India's IT giants to become Mahindra Satyam. Ironically, Ramalinga Raju later revealed that the deal to buy his sons' companies, which triggered the exposure of the scandal, was a desperate attempt to defend Satyam against a possible takeover, during which time the accounts would have been presented for inspection, by replacing the nonexistent assets on its books with genuine ones. There are also signs that problems in India's IT sector as the world economy hits stormier waters may not be limited to the Satyam fraud. Wipro, an even larger IT company, was banned from bidding for World Bank contracts in 2007 for bribing bank staff, a ban with another year still to run.

Stanford's Billions (2009)

Sir Allen Stanford maintains a
high profile and awaits trial
on charges of running the second
largest Ponzi scheme after
Bernard Madoff.

Background

R. Allen Stanford owned a chain of health clubs which went bankrupt in 1981. After working in a burger bar and without any banking experience, he opened his own bank on the Caribbean island of Monserrat in 1985, using money from property development. By offering depositors a return of two percent over normal bank rates, he attracted investors from all over Latin America, but in 1991 charges of involvement in money laundering caused his banking license to be revoked. Stanford moved to Antigua, and bought the Bank of Antigua, before opening his own Stanford International Bank. He continued to thrive, and donated to local causes, including building a cricket ground and a hospital. He was even knighted by the Antiguan Government.

Deception

As with Ponzi (see page 21) and Madoff (see page 39), the returns Stanford offered to investors seemed far too good to be true. But so high was his profile as a successful businessman, newspaper owner, backer of the Antiguan Government's debts, and sponsor of a hugely expensive world cricket series, that doubts remained muted. Allegations that all might not be well were defended strongly by the company and their own security team investigated the backgrounds of anyone who questioned the probity of Stanford's bank.

Exposure

Eventually, Stanford's traditional sources of investment in Latin America began to run dry, and he switched his banking services to US markets. There his high rates of return sparked off alarms in the wake of similar pyramid scandals like Ponzi's and Madoff's. Though the Stanford banks insisted all was well, experts said the basic math refused to add up. Both the IRS and FBI were watching Stanford International, one for missing tax returns and the other for signs of money laundering. One Drug Enforcement Administration investigation claimed drug money from Mexico found its way into the bank's reserves, but this claim was not pursued.

Meanwhile, Stanford's operation was still expanding. By 2007, it had increased its American network from 6 branches to more than 25, in cities like Boston and San Francisco as well as the Southern states. In 2004, Lester Bird, Prime Minister of Antigua and close friend of Stanford, lost his election. He was replaced by opposition politician Baldwin Spencer, who disliked Stanford. Even though he was underwriting so much Antiguan debt, the loss of political influence meant Stanford had also lost much of his company's security. Though workers within the Stanford operation were expressing concerns over how it was being run, by 2008, Stanford International claimed to be worth $8 billion in asset value.

Finally, in the closing months of 2008, the market plunged, and Madoff's fraud was exposed. Now Stamford's unrealistic claims of 30 percent deposit growth and better than 20 percent return on investments stood out in even sharper relief. On February 10, 2009, Laura Pendergest-Holt, Stanford's chief investment officer, told Security and Exchange Commission (SEC) officials in Fort Worth that she had no idea what the bank's most secret accounts actually contained. Searches revealed an apparent $2.5 billion shortfall, and on February 17, Federal agents raided Stanford's offices. A week later Pendergest-Holt was arrested for giving false information.

Fallout

The SEC froze the bank's assets as its main branches in Antigua and Venezuela were besieged by worried investors. Stanford was tracked down

Above Sir Allen Stanford appearing at Lord's Cricket Ground on June 11, 2008. Stanford and the English Cricket Board (ECB) announced a lucrative multi-million dollar deal for one-off cricket matches between England and a West Indian XI.

after two days to one of his houses in Virginia, and arrested on charges of fraudulently selling $8 billion worth of deposit certificates bearing impossibly high interest rates. Experts pointed out the bank's 30,000 customers in 131 different countries would lose the bulk of their funds, but public outcry seemed strangely subdued, perhaps because the majority of deposit holders were in Latin America. Stanford himself and his head of investments still deny any wrongdoing and insist the money is safe. Stanford also denies obstructing the SEC. He was taken into custody in June 2009, where he awaits trial.

BARINGS

Part Two:
Corporate Fraud

The Crédit Mobilier Scandal (1872)

The Union Pacific Railroad set up a fake company, Crédit Mobilier, to enable it to avoid US Government restrictions on profiteering.

Background

During the American railroad boom, the US Government realized companies would make millions operating completed routes and selling land alongside their tracks, so the governement limited the costs it would cover while the lines were being built. In 1867 this proved difficult for the Union Pacific Railroad, because it was extending its main line through the sparsely populated lands of Nebraska and Utah, so it devised a way to increase the amount it could charge to the government. It simply set up a fake sub-contracting company, called Crédit Mobilier, which would send in bills for the government to pay.

Above The railway bed of the unfinished Union Pacific Railroad, September 1866.

Deception

Crédit Mobilier was a deception both simple and effective, and also difficult to detect. It opened an office next door to that of the Union Pacific Railroad in Omaha, Nebraska, though it was supposed to be an entirely separate organization, chosen by Union Pacific to carry out all the construction work on its main line. Crédit Mobilier would send in bills for the work, which Union Pacific would approve, and then charge the US Government for reimbursement, adding only a small (and governement-approved) mark-up for its own overheads. Though the bills were much higher than the true construction costs, the government had no direct basis for comparison, and it was clear that Union Pacific was simply asking the government to meet its legitimate costs. Though it was against regulations, the arrangement was not actually illegal at the time.

Exposure

The only weakness in the scheme was that Union Pacific's construction contracts always went to Crédit Mobilier, without any real negotiation. Crédit Mobilier was making a lot of money on Southern Pacific construction, and so its share value rose sharply. Shares were sold to politicians at a massive discount to discourage anyone taking too close an interest in how the business was run. All went well until the Presidential election campaign of 1872. By that time control of Crédit Mobilier had passed to Oakes Ames, a Congressman from Massachusetts. *The New York Sun* newspaper had been sent incriminating letters by Henry Simpson McComb, a former associate of Ames who had disputes with him and who wanted to reveal the truth behind the deception. The letters showed that one contract had paid Crédit Mobilier a total of $72 million for construction work that had only cost $53 million. While shareholders in the false company had done very well, investors in Union Pacific had seen their company almost bankrupted.

Fallout

The fact that Ames was a congressman triggered a full Congressional investigation into what became known as the "Crédit Mobilier scandal." (Confusingly, a French bank after which the false company had been named collapsed not long before, so there were separate "Crédit Mobilier scandals" on both sides of the Atlantic.) Ames and other politicians who had benefited from the scam were censured, including the future president James Garfield, and false rumors of President Ulysses Grant's involvement partially tarnished his reputation.

Lockheed Bribery Scandals (1975)

American aircraft manufacturer
Lockheed developed a sure-fire
way to win contracts against
increasingly tough international
opposition; By bribing the decision makers.

Background
Modern aircraft, both civilian and military are hugely expensive to produce, so the whole future of a manufacturer can hang on the outcome of a contract with a country seeking to replace existing planes. As a result, the temptation to tilt the balance to win a vital order can be almost irresistible.

Deception
Lockheed suffered problems of increasing costs of developing the C5 transport in the late 1950s. Then the bankruptcy of Rolls Royce in 1971 (producer of the engines for its TriStar airliner) cost Lockheed $300 million in cancelled orders. In 1971 the US Government had to step in to help, by guaranteeing the repayment of $195 million in bank loans on the company's behalf. By August 1975 Lockheed was almost $1 billion in debt, and its solvency depended on selling 300 TriStars, a huge commercial target. However, it was more successful in gaining US Government contracts and in selling its aircraft overseas, even when its designs were closely matched and even exceeded by its competitors. The TriStar airliner was competing against the Douglas DC10, while the F-104 Starfighter was up against the French Mirage military jets, but contract after contract was won by Lockheed. No-one realized this success depended on large bribes paid in secret to those who awarded each contract in Lockheed's favor.

Exposure
In 1975 a Senate committee led by Senator Frank Church began questioning Lockheed executives about inducements paid to secure some of these lucrative

foreign contracts—at the time it was not actually against US law to make these payments, provided they were properly recorded in the accounts. To their surprise, it was revealed that the company had paid $22 million for sales of the F-104 Starfighter alone. Lockheed claimed that German Defence Minister, Franz-Josef Strauss, and his party had been paid $10 million to influence the sale of 900 Starfighters to the West German Luftwaffe. The German nickname for these planes was the "Widowmaker" because they had a dubious safety record in German service, so this claim was hugely controversial and strong denials were backed up by threats of legal action. However, the German Defence Ministry claimed the papers relating to the sale had been destroyed in 1962.

Both a former president and prime minister of Italy were forced to resign after details emerged of bribes paid to secure sales of the C-130 military transport. In Japan, Lockheed payments had secured orders for the Starfighter instead of the competitive Grumman F-11 Super Tiger. Furthermore, the $3 million that was given to Japanese prime minister Kakuei Tanaka, and the recruitment of Yoshio Kodama (a powerful underworld figure) to help their campaign, had resulted in All-Nippon Airways canceling its options to buy DC10 airliners and ordering 21 TriStars instead.

Fallout

The revelations spread still further. Prince Bernhard of the Netherlands was alleged to have accepted a bribe of $1.1 million to ensure the Dutch bought the F-104 instead of the French Mirage 5. Though he denied the allegations, interviews revealed after his death in 2004 that he had taken the bribe. When the scandal broke, Lockheed insisted that if these payments were not made, overseas competitors would simply pay bribes instead. It also maintained that revealing payments for contracts still in progress, to comply with US law, would risk losing those contracts. Nevertheless, Lockheed chairman Daniel J. Haughton and president Carl Kotchian resigned on February 13, 1976. On December 19, 1977 President Jimmy Carter introduced the Foreign Corrupt Practices Act to make future inducements completely illegal. Finally, in 1995, Lockheed merged with another leading plane-maker, the Martin Marietta corporation, to form Lockheed Martin.

The Recruit Scandal (1988)

A simple attempt to boost the value of a company's shares before stock exchange flotation caused the resignation of the Japanese Prime Minister, a suicide, and a change of government after 38 years of power.

Background

The Japanese company Cosmos was a subsidiary of the much larger Recruit information technology group with interests in property, telecommunications, and human resources operating in Tokyo in the 1980s. It was decided to offer Cosmos shares on public sale in 1986. Clearly if the value of the shares increased on its public flotation, then those who held large blocks of shares would make a great deal of money.

Deception

Recruit's founder and former chairman, Hiromasa Ezoe, wanted to head off a threatened Labor Ministry enquiry into his company and to increase its value by boosting the price of Cosmos shares. He mounted a classic insider-trading ploy by offering large numbers of Cosmos shares to 17 senior politicians and 150 leading businessmen at a fraction of their real value a month before they were offered to the public. The intention was to boost confidence in shares, stimulate further buying, and produce a spectacular rise in the company's share value. It was later estimated that all of the individuals in the deal made average profits of some 66 million yen each.

Exposure

The successful fraud was revealed by a local Japanese newspaper, which reported the trade-off between cut-price Cosmos stock and promises that the increased official supervision of Recruit's affairs would be scaled back. Growing public anger was fueled by revelations that many leading figures in Japanese public life were involved in the scandal.

Fallout

Later enquiries revealed that Ezoe was no stranger to paying politicians for favors; previously he had spent some 10 million yen to help the fundraising efforts of 50 members of the Japanese Diet or Parliament. Nevertheless, the list of high-level ministers and officials who had benefited from the share-dealing fraud was studded with famous names. These included the then Prime Minister of Japan, Noboru Takeshita, his predecessor in office Yasuhiro Nakasone, finance minister Kiichi Miyazawa, the Cabinet Secretary Takao Fujinami, and the Secretary-General of the ruling Liberal Democratic Party (LDP). The LDP had been in power for almost four decades, and the tightening mesh of corruption involved senior officials at the ministries of education and labor. Even the opposition parties, like the Democratic Socialist Party of Japan and the so-called Clean Party, were implicated in the scandal, as were leaders in telecommunications and newspaper publishing. Ezoe himself was forced to resign though was not charged with any offense. The Prime Minister was driven out of office, along with four members of his cabinet, his principal secretary committed suicide, and another 20 individuals were arrested. In the 1989 election, increased public hostility saw the LDP lose its majority in the Upper House of the Japanese parliament, and in the 1993 elections it was eventually voted out of office after 38 years in power. Widespread demands for political reform and higher ethical standards in public office still dominate debate in Japan, though the whole system depends on huge donations from businesses to keep cash-starved politicians and their parties functioning.

The Guinness Shares Scandal (1990)

The Guinness brewing company wanted to raise the funds for a costly takeover of the Scottish drinks group Distillers during the 1980s. They decided to boost the value of their company's shares by buying them in large quantities.

GUINNESS
is good for you

Background

Ernest Saunders, chief executive of the Irish brewers Guinness, was keen to move the company into the big league of drinks manufacturers by taking over the larger Distillers group. The Distillers board were happy to be taken over by Guinness, but there was a rival bid from the Argyll group, which meant the takeover carried a large £2.7 billion price tag, which was beyond Guinness' resources at the time.

Deception

Saunders and his associates, financier Jack Lyons, businessman Gerald Ronson, and City trader Anthony Parnes, decided the way to solve the problem was to boost the value of Guinness shares by fooling the market, buying shares as part of a concerted plan. Saunders had switched $100 million of Guinness money to US trader Ivan Boesky to buy and recommend Guinness shares. In addition, Saunders paid another $38 million to 11 different companies in half a dozen countries to stimulate trade in the company's shares, all without the knowledge of his board of directors. The deception worked very well, with Guinness shares trebling in value, and the planned takeover proceeding on schedule in April 1986.

Exposure

Saunders was praised for his vision and acumen, but the whole deception came crashing down in December 1986 when Ivan Boesky was arrested in the US for alleged insider dealing. As part of a plea bargain, he told the Securities and Exchange Commission (SEC) about the cash used to buttress dealings in Guinness shares to fund the takeover. The SEC passed the information on to the UK Department of Trade and Industry, who began a detailed enquiry into the whole takeover and share trading. One of Saunders' fellow conspirators, Olivier Roux, a Boston management consultant loaned to the Guinness financial department, was granted immunity from prosecution in exchange for inside information. Roux wrote to the Guinness board to tell them of the scheme and they responded by firing Saunders in January 1987.

Fallout

Saunders, Lyons, Parnes, and Ronson were put on trial in February 1990. At the end of one of the longest and most expensive fraud trials in British legal history (lasting for 100 days and costing some £18 million), all four were found guilty of theft and false accounting. Saunders was sentenced to five years in jail, though this was halved on appeal after his claims he was suffering from Alzheimer's disease, a normally incurable brain disorder. Lyons was deprived of his knighthood and fined £4 million, while Ronson was jailed for a year and fined £5 million, and Parnes had a 30-month sentence cut to 21 months on appeal. Though all the defendants spent a great deal of time trying to have their convictions overturned and their names cleared, the original verdicts were upheld, though Saunders' rapid and lasting recovery from Alzheimer's disease following his release from prison caused widespread public cynicism.

WorldCom Bankruptcy Fraud (1992)

A sharp downturn in the telecommunications market hit the giant WorldCom corporation particularly hard: A crisis which led them to bankruptcy.

Background

Based in Clinton, Mississippi, WorldCom was one of the most spectacular success stories in the booming US telecommunications sector during the 1990s. Founded as Long Distance Discount Services (LDDS) in 1983 by chief executive Bernard Ebbers, it had shown continuous growth through to the late 1990s, with a series of takeovers making it the second largest telecommunications company behind AT&T.

Deception

Problems began mounting in 1999, when the company's costly $129 million planned takeover deal of its competitor, the Sprint Corporation, was vetoed by industry regulators, at a time when the declining economy meant that customers were reducing their telecommunications expenditure. Debts were mounting so Ebbers worked with Scott Sullivan, his chief financial officer, and two other directors to change the accounts to suggest the company was more profitable than it was. They shifted interconnection costs with other telecommunication companies from their expenses account to their capital account, causing the company's expenses to appear smaller than they actually were, and they made the income look larger by adding false entries from what they described as "corporate unallocated revenue accounts." The effect of these changes was to make the company's financial position billions of dollars better than it was.

Exposure

Ebbers was taking other precautions to meet his financial obligations, mainly from banks that were concerned about the company stock he was using to prop up his other businesses. In 2001, he persuaded the board to lend him more than $400 million in loans and guarantees, but as the company's share price fell, he was replaced as chief executive in April 2002. When a team of internal auditors examined the WorldCom books, they found that they had been cooked by almost $4 billion. The board fired Ebbers' co-conspirators, and the US Securities and Exchange Commission (SEC) began an investigation on June 26, 2002. They found the company's assets had been boosted by $11 billion in all.

Fallout

In July 2002 the company filed for bankruptcy under Chapter 11 rules, which allowed it to continue trading until a solution was found. Two years later, it was merged with MCI, a subsidiary of Verizon Communications, and moved to Ashburn, Virginia, before a final change of name to Verizon Business in 2006. As part of the bankruptcy reorganization, the company agreed to pay $750 million to the SEC in cash and stock in MCI, to allow investors to be repaid their losses resulting from the fraud. In March 2005 Ebbers, together with his fellow conspirators, was found guilty of fraud, conspiracy, and filing false documents, which in his case meant serving a 25-year prison sentence.

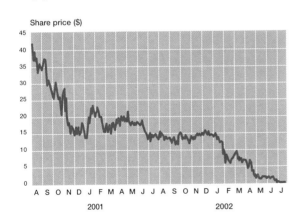

Above A graph showing the steep decrease in value of WorldCom shares until its eventual bankruptcy in July 2002.

The Barings Bank Cover-up (1995)

In the exotic and fast-moving world of currency trading brokers can make a mistake and cause their employers stupendous losses, so they face real temptation to cover up their mistakes until they can find a winning streak.

BARINGS

Background

Nick Leeson had joined Barings Bank (the UK's oldest established investment bank) in 1989 at the age of 22, after working at Coutts and Morgan Stanley. His application for a broker's license in the City of London was turned down because a fraud had been discovered on his application. Barings then sent him to manage futures trading in their Singapore office, where he carried out a hugely successful series of deals on the Singapore International Monetary Exchange. By correctly predicting market and currency movements in 1992, for example, he had earned Barings £10 million, representing 10 percent of the bank's income for the year, which brought him a bonus of £130,000 on top of his £50,000 annual salary. But by January 2005, his luck had run out, and he was incurring massive and increasing losses.

Deception

There was one way to hide his problems until his luck changed. This was to use an "error account," a special account set up to correct mistakes made in the ordinary course of trading. For example, when one of his colleagues had sold 20 new contracts instead of buying them as ordered by a customer, she had cost Barings £20,000, and the losses were hidden away in the error account. Apart from the fact that Leeson's failure to obtain a broker's license in London had been kept secret, his job had another unusual feature. He not only worked as a trader, but was also responsible for settling the trades he had made, roles normally carried out by two different people to keep tighter control on trading operations. This was ideal for someone wanting to hide his losses. By early 1993, these hidden shortfalls amounted to £2 million, and over the following two years this hidden debt ballooned to £208 million, and the situation continued to spiral out of control.

Exposure

On January 16, 1995, Leeson set up what brokers called a "short straddle" in both the Singapore and Tokyo stock exchanges, which essentially meant he was risking Baring's money on his prediction that the Japanese stock market would remain relatively steady overnight. Though he had no way of knowing this in advance, this would be the worst night of all to make this kind of prediction as the Japanese city of Kobe suffered a catastrophic earthquake in the early hours, causing the stock market to plunge. On its own, this was bad enough, but Leeson compounded his error by risking still more money on his prediction that the Nikkei average—an index of the value of leading shares on the Japanese stock exchange —would recover quickly from the steep falls caused by news of the earthquake. It did not, and Leeson was now powerless to

Above The city of Kobe was Japan's most important port. The devastation caused by the earthquake killed thousands and left stock markets reeling around the globe.

cover his catastrophic performance. On February 23, 1995 he fled Singapore for Malaysia, and then crossed into Thailand before finally flying to hide out in Germany.

Fallout

Leeson's position was grim, but that of Barings Bank was even worse. Losses resulting from his mistakes eventually reached a staggering £827 million, roughly twice the bank's entire trading capital. It ceased trading just three days after Leeson left his office with a note of apology, and was finally sold to a Netherlands banking group for just £1. Leeson himself was extradited to Singapore to face fraud charges for not warning his employers of the risks he was taking and the losses he was accumulating. He blamed the bank's lax management, effectively for letting him get away with it. He was sentenced to six and a half years in jail, only to be released in 1999 after being diagnosed with bowel cancer.

Above Nick Leeson arriving at Singapore's Changi airport, November 23, after being extradited from Germany.

The Air Canada Airbus Affair (1995)

The European Airbus had an uphill
struggle competing for sales
against competition from the
larger and longer established
makers like Boeing, and once again
the problem of illegal payments
to secure sales was suspected.

Background

During the 1980s, Boeing and Airbus Industries had been competing to win
a large and lucrative contract for Air Canada's airliner fleet. Boeing spent a
large amount of money to buy the de Havilland Canada company, as a way
of strengthening their hand and also to find themselves a foothold in the
future feeder-airliner market. Ironically, Airbus Industries had as its chairman
the German politician Franz-Josef Strauss who had been implicated in the
Lockheed bribery scandal (see page 52).

Deception

In 1988 the contract was finally awarded in favor of Airbus, with an order for 34
Airbus A320s, and the sale of some of the Air Canada Boeing 747 fleet. Boeing
reacted by selling de Havilland Canada, which had a damaging effect on the
company and on the Canadian jobs it represented, all of which made any
possibility of bribery even more damaging. Yet there were persistent allegations
of payments being made by Airbus to the then Canadian Prime Minister Brian
Mulroney to secure the contract, though this has always been denied.

Exposure

In 1995, the Royal Canadian Mounted Police wrote to the Swiss Government
asking for access to banking records. The letter explained that Karlheinz

Schreiber, a businessman and political lobbyist with dual Canadian-German citizenship, had not only helped underwrite Brian Mulroney's ultimately successful bid for the leadership of the Progressive Conservative Party, but had paid the prime minister large cash amounts in return for his role in securing the adoption of the A320 for Air Canada rather than its Boeing rival.

Fallout

Mulroney denied the allegations, and launched a CAD $50 million lawsuit against the Canadian Government, insisting that the Liberal administration under Premier Jean Chrétien, which had taken over from his own in 1993, was now seeking revenge by making false accusations. Significantly, the government backed down and apologized, paying Mulroney's legal fees of more than $2 million. Yet the affair continues to rumble on with no apparent end in sight. In 2003 it was admitted that Mulroney had accepted three cash payments of CAD $75,000 each over a year and a half to help promote a new pasta business and develop international contacts for Schreiber. Schreiber responded by saying the only work done for his pasta business was sending out a single publicity flyer. Then the Canadian Broadcasting Corporation put out a 1995 documentary alleging Airbus links with a Lichtenstein-based company, International Aircraft Leasing, which had been paid millions of dollars after the Air Canada order, and there were rumors of a mysterious Swiss bank account code-named "Britan."

Finally, a public enquiry was set up in November 2007 to examine the allegations. Schreiber, facing extradition to Germany for fraud and bribery charges, revealed he had paid Mulroney CAD $300,000 in 2007 from commission received from several European companies, including Airbus Industries. Mulroney himself appeared before the enquiry but withdrew insisting that he was being treated unfairly. The enquiry closed without reaching any conclusions. Since then, the formation of the Oliphant Commission in April 2009 has reopened the whole question of payments between Schreiber and Mulroney.

Robbing the Shareholders (2005)

Canadian newspaper tycoon Conrad Black became Baron Black of Crossharbour, but was convicted of milking his companies to fund an increasingly lavish lifestyle.

Background

Conrad Black was a successful newspaper publisher. By the early 1990s, his Hollinger group owned 60 percent of all Canadian papers and papers in the US, Israel, Australia, and UK. In 1985, he bought the London *Daily Telegraph* and in 1994 followed this with the *Chicago Sun-Times*. By 1999, the company's annual turnover was more than $2 billion, and he was spending more of his time in London, where he had been proposed for a life peerage (a non-hereditary title) while Hollinger International shares had been listed on the New York Stock Exchange. In 2001, he became Lord Black, but to overcome a Canadian ban on citizens accepting foreign honors, he had to become a British citizen.

Deception

Already stories had circulated about Black's earliest business dealings, from his buying General Motors shares at the age of eight to his being expelled from school for selling illicit examination papers to fellow pupils. However, as time passed, more serious concerns arose. Shareholders suspected that Black's ultra-lavish lifestyle, with private jets and expensive homes in London, Toronto, Palm Beach, and Manhattan, was increasingly at odds with the fortunes of Hollinger International, now showing signs of stagnation.

Exposure

In 2003, reacting to shareholder concerns, the Hollinger board appointed a committee to check the accounts. They found what they called "excessive" fees paid to Black and some of his fellow directors, and they immediately demanded repayment. In early 2004 the Hollinger board sacked Black and sued him for $200 million for false accounting to divert money to his own personal accounts. Resisting demands for repayment, Black countersued. He also tried to sell several of his most successful papers to the UK Barclay brothers, but this move was blocked by the Hollinger board. Finally, on August 31, 2004, the US Securities and Exchange Commission (SEC) issued a damning report on the findings of the Hollinger committee which said Black had run his company "like a corporate kleptocracy," joining with fellow directors to help themselves to hundreds of millions of dollars of company funds.

Fallout

Events soon went from bad to worse. In November 2005 the US charged him with mail fraud and wire fraud in the diversion of company funds. Later

charges of racketeering, obstruction of justice, money laundering, and tax evasion were added. Black denied all these charges and mounted a vigorous but expensive legal challenge, the soaring costs of which forced him to sell many of his shareholdings and two of his homes, and to mortgage a third. Finally, in July 2007 a Chicago court sentenced him to six and a half years in jail for mail fraud and obstruction of justice. Following repeated appeals, in May 2009 the US Supreme Court agreed to review his fraud conviction, and a ruling is expected in June 2010, though his obstruction of justice conviction is not covered by the appeal.

Above Conrad Black leaves the federal courthouse with his wife Barbara Amiel following his bail hearing on August 1, 2007

The Chinese Pensions Scandal (2006)

The colossal Shanghai pensions fund scandal, where a third was sold off to fund risky toll-road and property investment projects, showed the dark side of China's economic boom.

Background

Shanghai's social security fund manages more than $1.4 billion worth of assets to provide its citizens' pensions. Like all major public institutions in China, it is run by the Communist Party, but because a continuing economic boom offered huge returns for anyone able to invest in a succession of large-scale new projects, it became a huge temptation for anyone wanting to join the scramble for riches.

Deception

The man behind the racket was the Shanghai local Communist Party chief and Politburo member, Chen Liangyu. Over an eight-year period from 1998, the fraudsters diverted some $400,000 from the pension funds' normal low-risk but low-return investments into highly speculative toll road and property developments offering them much faster and larger returns. The fraud involved diverting funds from public sources, so it had to avoid alerting too many officials. Those who became aware of the fraud had to be bribed to keep quiet, using even more of the pension funds to buy their silence.

Exposure

No details have emerged on how the scandal was first brought to light. One possibility is that when current Chinese President Hu Jintao succeeded his predecessor Jiang Zemin, he found Jiang had surrounded himself with officials from his own home city of Shanghai. When they were replaced with officials loyal to himself, President Hu may have uncovered details of the fraud. He set in motion a massive official enquiry, where more than 100 official investigators found some $425 million missing from the pension fund accounts. The trail went straight to Chen Liangyu's office, though it soon led to other Party officials and heads of commercial companies. In 2006 Chen was expelled from the Party, and charged with investing millions of dollars worth of pension fund assets in shaky investments, shielding corrupt colleagues, helping out illegal businesses, and abusing his position on behalf of members of his family. He was put on trial, and on April 11, 2008 was sentenced to 18 years in jail for abuse of power, stock manipulation, financial fraud, and accepting $340,000 in bribes from corrupt business operators. He was the most senior Party official to be punished for corruption in more than ten years.

Fallout

This was just the beginning: It soon became clear how far the corruption had spread through the city's commercial and political elite. The manager of the city's Formula One racing circuit, the director of the Shanghai Asset Supervision Board, and the deputy director who administered Shanghai housing land and resources were all fired. China's chief statistician was also relieved of his duties, either for failing to identify the fraud or for trying to cover it up. The District Governor was also dismissed, as was the chief of the labor and social security organization. Hong Kong newspapers reported more than 50 businessmen and government officials had been arrested. The Chinese leadership put in a new management team to deal with the loss of some $475 million, or one third of the pension funds, and official reports claim the bulk of the money has been recovered and any shortfall made good. One unexpected effect of the scandal has been the spectacular rise in popularity of an online game called "Incorruptible Fighter" in which players can torture and eliminate corrupt officials while helping honest ones, using well-known characters from Chinese history to win through to a corruption-free paradise. So high was the demand that the game's website crashed after it had been downloaded more than 100,000 times.

Jérôme Kerviel and Société Général (2008)

France's "rogue trader" scandal
resulted from a keen bank
employee evading its own
security system with extremely
bad timing, turning a potential
profit into huge losses.

Background

Jérôme Kerviel worked in Paris for the French bank Société Générale. After
studying finance at the universities of Nantes and Lyon, he joined the bank in
2000. He was appointed a junior trader in March 2005, at a fairly low basic
salary of 74,000 euros for such a high-powered operation. Kerviel soon
established a reputation as a quiet and taciturn professional, loth to take the
holidays due to him and apparently completely devoted to his job.

Deception

When he correctly predicted a falling market during 2007, he made more
than $2 billion worth of profit by the end of the year. This persuaded him
to gamble with higher and higher sums. To avoid revealing that he was
exceeding his credit limit, Kerviel posted fake loss-making deals to suggest
he was still within financial limits. By closing trades quickly, he ensured the
bank's timed security controls remained unaware of what he was doing. He
would then replace these deals with new ones. As conditions changed and his
losses grew, Société Générale remained unaware of what was really happening.
Even when security checks revealed anomalies he convinced his bosses a
simple mathematical error had been responsible and that everything was
under control.

Exposure

The true state of affairs was revealed on Friday, January 18, 2008, after Kerviel left his office to return to his apartment in Neuilly-sur-Seine. Not anticipating problems, he had failed to close his current deals, at the very moment when the market began a spectacular fall. Bank officials called him to tell him a problem had appeared with one of his trades, and summon him to a meeting to explain. But by early on the Sunday morning, it was clear his secret deals on a plunging market had exposed the bank to losses that could reach tens of billions of euros and potentially close it down. By six that evening, all his deals had been identified and were being closed as quickly as possible. To avoid panic spreading the bank informed

Above Jérôme Kerviel (bottom) in a 2001 electoral leaflet, where he was standing as a candidate for election to the local council of his home town Pont l'Abbé in Brittany.

the French financial regulatory authorities, but not the government. Had the market rallied, this speedy action to remedy the situation would have been successful, but conditions were rapidly worsening. By the middle of the week, Société Générale's position had been stabilized and the immediate danger was over, but at the price of losses totaling billions of euros.

Fallout

By the following Friday, the bank had charged Kerviel with using fake and fraudulent documents and tampering with its own security systems. French police raided the bank's offices and Kerviel's apartment. On January 26 he was questioned before being charged with "abuse of confidence and illegal access to computers." It soon became clear the situation was more complex than it seemed—had Kerviel closed his deals on December 31, he would not have lost the bank any money at all, but instead would have made it a substantial profit. Up to that time, he still expected a 2008 bonus of 600,000 euros on top of his salary, from a 60 million euro profit on his trading.

Since then, skeptics have insisted the bank has tried to cover up inadequate security systems, and used Kerviel as a scapegoat to hide massive losses in areas where he had no responsibility. The bank's chairman, Daniel Bouton, was forced to resign over his handling of the problem. Kerviel himself has insisted he was merely trying to make money for his employers and that he personally made no money at all from his dealing. He was jailed until March 2008 and then released on condition he remains well away from the banking industry, though he still faces potential charges of fraud and abuse of trust. So far, evidence remains a problem, but he could still face a fine of more than 3 million euros and up to five years in prison.

The Hong Kong Share Fraud (2009)

Potential takeovers usually have to be approved by shareholders, but creating new and compliant shareholders amounts to a simple case of fraud.

Background

Prominent Hong Kong businessman Richard Li wanted his telecommunications company, Pacific Century CyberWorks (PCCW), to be taken over by the state-controlled mobile phone company, China Unicom. He had bought the company for $28.5 billion in 2000, and having tried several times to sell it as its value had dropped sharply, he was concerned that the company's shareholders might vote to block the deal, especially since the proposed 60 cents US price per share would be seen as severely undervaluing their holdings.

Deception

Francis Yuen, a senior associate of Mr. Li, would later be accused of ordering Lam Hau Wah, a regional director at Fortis Insurance Asia, to help prevent a veto from happening. Fortis Insurance was linked to another of Mr. Li's companies, Pacific Century Insurance Holdings. Mr. Lam was to distribute 1,000 PCCW shares each to 500 employees, along with orders to take part in the forthcoming vote. Not surprisingly, 494 of those given shares voted in favor of the takeover and it appeared this would then proceed without further delay.

Exposure

David Webb, described as a "well-known corporate governance and investment commentator" and a prominent critic of the way in which shareholders' interests tend to be ignored by big businesses in Hong Kong, was sent an anonymous e-mail informing him that PCCW shares were being offered to outsiders, if they voted in favor of the offer. Preliminary investigations had been made into the PCCW shareholder list and it had been found that on a random sample there were a large number of new shareholders whose names happened to correspond with existing names of Fortis Insurance agents. Webb alerted the Hong Kong authorities and the Securities and Futures Commission (SFC) carried out an investigation. This revealed recordings of telephone conversations between Mr. Yuen and Mr. Lam and also found that Mr. Yuen's secretary had been preparing proxy voting forms at his office and passing them on to Mr. Lam's secretary. Nevertheless, Richard Li, PCCW, Fortis Insurance, and Pacific Century Insurance all issued strong denials of any involvement and there was no firm evidence directly linking them to the deception.

Fallout

An action was brought by shareholders' groups to block the takeover proposal. Justice Kwan decided that it was impossible for the court to decide whether or not share manipulation had taken place, and that even if it had, there was no need for the court to intervene. Nor did the judge consider there was any real link between Mr. Yuen and Mr. Lam beyond a series of coincidences.

Opponents of the takeover then took the case to the Court of Appeal where the decision was reversed on May 11, 2009, on the grounds that the scheme was "clear manipulation." Justice Rogers went further, declaring that "vote manipulation is nothing less than a form of dishonesty. The court cannot sanction dishonesty." He also noted that Mr. Lam had bought 2.4 million PCCW shares in the first half of January, the first he had bought for ten years, and had subsequently withdrawn half a million of them in lots of 1,000 apiece, which were then distributed among the company's agents as a bonus. In fact, the SFC analysis showed that there were 335 genuine agents who received shares, but others went to secretaries, clerks, spouses, and various acquaintances, including a babysitter and a tailor. Furthermore, the voting figures showed that almost all of the votes against the takeover proposal were from long-term shareholders, whereas almost all those who voted in its favor had been given shares after the takeover had been announced. The three appeal judges unanimously blocked the proposal, and on the following day it was dropped.

Part Three:

Cover-ups
and Deceptions

Watergate (1974)

On June 17, 1972 when Republican
President Richard Nixon was
preparing his campaign for
reelection for a second term
in office, a team of burglars
was caught inside the offices
of the Democratic Party's National
Committee in Washington's Watergate Hotel.

Background
What seemed at first to be a straightforward case of theft was soon revealed
to be much more significant. *The Washington Post* revealed that the break-in
team were carrying large amounts of cash and wearing surgical gloves, and
that one—James McCord—was a member of the Republican Party and on
the committee working for the President's reelection.

Deception
Within hours, pressure was being mounted by the White House to order the
CIA to persuade the FBI to drop its investigation into the case. It was later
revealed that two former members of Nixon's White House team, former FBI
agent Gordon Liddy and CIA officer Howard Hunt, had been hiding in a
hotel room opposite the Watergate building during the break-in, communicating
with the burglars by two-way radio to guide them over what to look for at
the scene.

Exposure
So far, there was nothing to link the burglary directly to President Nixon,
even though there seemed to be several clear links between the break-in and
the White House. The breakthrough emerged when *Washington Post* reporter
Carl Bernstein found out that a cheque for $25,000 made out to Nixon's

Above August 8th 1974: American President Richard Nixon announces his resignation on national television, following the Watergate Scandal.

reelection campaign had been deposited in the bank account of one of the burglars, by way of Nixon's chief fundraiser. This was soon followed by revelations that the US Attorney General, a Nixon appointee, controlled a covert fund which was targeted at gathering sensitive information on Democrat opponents, and that members of the President's staff had run a concerted campaign of sabotage and information gathering aimed at the opposition party. But for the time being, the rest of the American press continued to leave this sensitive story alone, and Nixon was reelected by an increased majority in November 1972. Meanwhile the *Washington Post* continued to be attacked by the White House for what it described as biased and misleading coverage, and the paper's publishers were the target of a campaign of threats and harassment.

Fallout

In February 1973 the Senate set up two committees to investigate the whole Watergate controversy. As witnesses began to give evidence in public, the whole cover-up began to unravel. White House aide John Dean alleged that the President knew all about plans to deny knowledge of the burglary. Then, in July 1973 another insider told the enquiry that Nixon had taped all phone calls and conversations in his office. The enquiry demanded copies of the tapes but at first the President refused. When the matter threatened to reach the Supreme Court, the White House agreed to release written transcripts of the tapes. One prosecutor accepted this deal, the other rejected it and was promptly fired by Nixon as a result. Increasing numbers of the President's team were dismissed to deflect attention from the man at the top, as calls grew for him to be impeached.

Finally, in April 1974 Nixon released 1,200 pages of transcripts, which contained many references to raising money to pay off potential blackmailers and concealing evidence of perjury. One transcript in particular, relating to a conversation of June 23, 1972, revealed that Nixon had known all about the cover-up to the Watergate burglary and he was forced to step down to avoid the impeachment process being set in motion. He announced his resignation on August 8, 1974, and was replaced by Vice President Gerald Ford, who pardoned Nixon a month later. But the lasting legacy of the Watergate scandal was a new and much deeper suspicion of the Federal Government as a whole, and the Presidency in particular among the American public. Future Presidents would have to be aware that their actions and communications would come under much closer scrutiny.

Rainbow Warrior (1985)

In 1985, Greenpeace's support ship was blown up in a New Zealand harbor by French intelligence agents.

GREENPEACE

Background

The environmental activist group Greenpeace used the ship the *Rainbow Warrior* to support a range of high-profile protests against activities such as whaling and seal culling. In 1985, the ship was part of a campaign to disrupt the French nuclear test program at Mururoa Atoll in French Polynesia. The ship called at New Zealand to assemble a flotilla of yachts to sail into the test area, from which shipping had been excluded, and provoke confrontation.

Deception

Greenpeace also planned to place protesters on the test island to monitor any environmental damage. French intelligence agents had infiltrated the Canadian part of the organization, and knew of its intentions. The *Rainbow Warrior* was moored in Auckland Harbor in New Zealand before leaving for the tests, and had been open to the public, which let French agents examine the ship and plan her sinking. A small limpet mine was fixed to the hull, set to detonate at around 11:45 PM on July 10, 1985, causing the ship to be evacuated, and a larger mine set for ten minutes later to sink it. Both charges detonated on schedule, but the crew reboarded the ship to film the damage, and one cameraman drowned as it foundered. With supreme cynicism, the French Government joined the international outcry at the sinking, blaming it on international terrorism.

Exposure

Only two of the French agents were caught, Dominique Prieur and Alain Mafart, and they pleaded guilty to manslaughter, receiving ten years each. The French Government demanded their release, threatening a Europe-wide trade embargo to cripple New Zealand's economy. But in June 1986 the

French agreed to pay New Zealand some $6.5 million compensation on condition the two prisoners were allowed to serve three years at a French military base on Hao atoll, though they were both released after less than two years. Three other agents had escaped on a yacht, but were arrested by the Australians as they called at Norfolk Island. Unable to hold them long enough to test them for exposure to explosives, the Australians had to let them go, to be picked up by a French submarine, which sank their yacht before departing.

Fallout

A French enquiry exonerated the government, but Defence Minister Charles Hernu resigned and Admiral Lacoste, head of the French foreign intelligence service, was dismissed. New Zealand's own antinuclear policy was firmly entrenched following the incident and Greenpeace was paid $8.16 million in compensation. Twenty years later the French finally admitted President Mitterrand had approved the operation. Greenpeace still wants to extradite the commander of the operation, Louis-Pierre Dillais, from his home in the US.

Above Greenpeace ship the *Rainbow Warrior* in the Bay of Auckland, New Zealand.

The Iran–Contra Affair (1986)

The complex Iran-Contra scandal involved the US secretly selling arms to Iran, and using the money to buy more weapons for American-backed Contra rebels against the left-wing Sandinista regime in Nicaragua.

Background

What was later described as the greatest American political scandal since Watergate (see page 76) began in 1985 as an attempt to release six US hostages captured in Lebanon by the terrorist group Hezbollah. The group was supported by Iran, then at war with Iraq but starved of weapons under a strict arms embargo. In a complex deal, the Israelis would ship TOW (Tube-launched, Optically-tracked, Wire-guided) anti-tank missiles and Hawk anti-aircraft missiles through an intermediary to an influential group of Iranian moderates, who would then apply pressure to persuade Hezbollah to agree a deal to free the captives. The Israelis would be resupplied by the US, who would then be repaid the money released by the Iranians to pay for the missiles. Unfortunately, this was eventually seen as a straightforward case of selling arms to buy the release of hostages, against existing US doctrine governing negotiations with terrorists or their sponsors.

Deception

This was bad enough, but under the same heavy cloak of secrecy more deals were afoot. Colonel Oliver North of the National Security Council wished to provide weapons for another group America wanted to back. The winning of power by the Sandinista administration in Nicaragua, in the US backyard of Central America, made the Reagan White House sympathetic to the Contra opposition groups operating in that country. Giving them direct assistance would breach the terms of several decisions taken by Congress during the early 1980s. However, since the Iran deal and the payments were secret, this allowed Colonel North to suggest a change in the plans on December 5, 1985. By supplying future consignments directly to the Iranian group, the US could mark up the price and the extra funds would be channeled to supply weapons to the Contras, to help overturn the Sandinista regime.

Exposure

The secrecy was finally uncovered by a story in a Lebanese magazine *Ash-Shiraa*, which published details of the weapons-for-hostages trade on November 3, 1986. To make matters worse, an aircraft carrying American-

Above Contra rebels in training at a base on the border between Nicaragua and Honduras and Colonel North, one of the men considered to be responsible for the scandal.

supplied weapons to the Contras was brought down over Nicaraguan territory and some of the crew captured, revealing alleged links to the CIA. Within three weeks of the story's appearance, Colonel North began hiding some of the incriminating documents relating to the arms deals and destroying others, including official documents from the White House. So rushed was the destruction that the government shredder used to destroy the papers jammed under the amount of paper being forced through it. On November 25, 1986, President Reagan was compelled to admit to a news conference that funds obtained from supplying weapons to Iran in breach of the arms embargo had been used to buy weapons for the Contras, in defiance of the Senate's own restrictions. But he firmly denied he had known anything about the deals.

Fallout

Reagan named two people as responsible for the deals: Colonel North and National Security Advisor John M. Poindexter. In response to the enormous public unrest, two commissions of enquiry were set up: one by Congress, and the three-man Tower Committee by the President. Neither found any direct evidence that the President had first-hand knowledge of what his staff had been doing, though Poindexter resigned and North was dismissed. The public reaction was overwhelming skepticism that Reagan knew as little as he pretended, and his approval ratings dipped spectacularly, though they recovered to their previous level by the time his second term was over. Only four of the hostages were released as a result of the deal, and another Islamist group immediately seized another three Americans to restore their bargaining power.

The Marcos Dictatorship (1986)

Ferdinand Marcos studied to
become a lawyer while in prison
on murder charges—after his
acquittal, he was elected
President of the Philippines
but was mired in corruption and
electoral fraud until deposed and exiled.

Background

Ferdinand Marcos was convicted of murdering a political rival of his family in
the autumn of 1939 and sentenced to death at the age of 22. Following an
appeal, he was acquitted a year later. He used his prison time to study for the
Bar and later became a successful barrister. Following the Japanese invasion of
the Philippines in 1942, he claimed to have become leader of a guerrilla band
in the north of the island of Luzon and after the war he entered politics. After
three terms in the House of Representatives, he was elected as a Senator in
1959 and as President in 1965.

Deception

Marcos remained in power for 21 years. At first, he appeared to want to
improve prosperity and security for the people, but his administration soon
descended into virtual dictatorship, with massive corruption, political
repression, and violation of human rights. Political opponents and anyone
who criticized his rule risked extreme retaliation. Human rights groups
estimate at least 1,500 people were murdered during the years of martial law
and some 800 others simply disappeared without a trace. Sources within the
country also claim 120,000 people were arrested and imprisoned without
charges or trial. In addition, increasingly large amounts of public funds were
being diverted into the Marcos family's accounts and he was the subject of an

increasingly harsh and strident personality cult, maintained by those who had benefited from his favors and support.

Exposure

By 1983, Marcos' health was failing and his grip on power loosened by several absences from office with kidney problems. One physician dealing with his case claimed he had been given a kidney transplant; the doctor was murdered soon afterward, though his killer was never tracked down. New and more formidable challengers for the Presidency were winning growing public support. His closest political rival was Benigno Aquino, but before he could fight an election, Aquino was assassinated, and Marcos was heavily implicated in the killing. Though his involvement in the murder was never proven, the killing triggered an explosion of anger and discontent. With US support declining, Marcos was suddenly more vulnerable, and to strengthen his grip on power he called a hurried election in 1986, when his current term still had a year to run. Aquino's widow Corazon ran against him, and when the votes had all been counted, the official election monitors showed she had won by 800,000 votes. Marcos' supporters declared the margin was twice as large, but in the other direction. Anger at the attempted electoral fraud boiled over into revolution, and eventually the army changed sides and Marcos was deposed.

Fallout

Marcos and his wife Imelda—famous for her vast collection of shoes—were exiled to the US, but the couple had all but bankrupted their country. Their baggage included 24 suitcases filled with gold bullion, while billions of dollars had been stored in secret bank accounts, many in monopolies set up by Marcos during his time in power. Critics say the Philippines will be paying interest on the huge debts run up by the Marcos administration for years to come. Marcos himself died in 1989 and his widow returned to Philippines politics. Estimates for the number of people to have disappeared during his time in power vary from 750 to more than 100,000.

Disaster at Chernobyl (1986)

A safety test that went wrong caused massive explosions at the Chernobyl nuclear power station in 1986, scattering radioactive fallout over most of Europe.

Background

On April 25, 1986, reactor number 4 at Chernobyl was being shut down for routine maintenance, and it was decided to perform an overdue safety test. The reactor needed 45,000 tons of cooling water an hour, but an external power failure could trigger an automatic shut-down, cutting off power to the cooling water pumps. Back-up diesel generators took almost a minute to run up to full speed, so power from the main generator was needed to bridge the gap: This was the feature to be tested.

Deception

Unfortunately, a failure at another local power station postponed the shut down of reactor 4, so the final stages involved the inadequately briefed night shift. An engineer shut the reactor down below the power level needed for the test, so the control rods that damped down the nuclear reaction were withdrawn to allow power to increase. Because this happened slowly, more and more control rods were withdrawn, but to prevent the automatic safety devices from shutting the reactor down and stopping the test, these were disabled. At 1:23 on the morning of April 26, 1986, the test finally began, but within seconds the nuclear reaction was out of control. Just 36 seconds into the test, the operators tried to reinsert the control rods to stop the reactor. This took 20 seconds, but within seven seconds the reactor was already running at ten times normal power and the heat was distorting the control rods, preventing them from moving further, while producing huge quantities of steam. Finally, just 20 seconds later, a massive explosion blew off the 2,000 ton reactor roof, followed two or three seconds later by another explosion, and a release of radioactive material some four hundred times that of the Hiroshima bomb.

Exposure

At first the Soviets tried to cover up the explosions. The reactor was not sealed in a massive containment vessel like most Western nuclear reactors. It also later emerged that this crucial safety test had never before been carried out at Chernobyl, though official records had been falsified to say it had. The day after the explosions, workers at the Forsmark nuclear power station in Sweden, more than 600 miles away, found radiation traces on their clothing. Checks revealed the source of this mysterious radiation was in the Ukraine and slowly news emerged from the Soviet blackout.

Fallout

It took two weeks of helicopters dropping more than 5,000 tons of inert materials like sand and clay on to the reactor to finally put out the fires. To prevent the hot reactor sinking down into the water table, the soil beneath it was kept frozen at—100ºC by injecting it with 25 tons of liquid nitrogen each day. By December, the reactor had finally been sealed in a concrete casing. Thirty-one station and emergency workers died of radiation poisoning in the first three months and a total of 135,000 people were evacuated from the area. After concerns over worldwide contamination receded, Soviet officials were forced to institute stricter safety measures at its nuclear plants, and maintain a more open attitude to reporting any problems.

Maxwell and the Missing Pensions (1991)

Robert Maxwell was a war hero and successful publisher, but he systematically robbed his employees' pension funds.

Background

Robert Maxwell was born Jan Ludvik Hoch in what was then Czechoslovakia. Having lost most of his family to the Nazis, he escaped to England, where he joined the British Army, changed his name, and was awarded a commission and the Military Cross. Elected to Parliament as Labour MP for Buckingham, he also became a successful publisher and newspaper owner.

Deception

In 1969 Maxwell falsely claimed that one of his companies was extremely profitable to boost its sale price and the Department of Trade and Industry reported that in their opinion he was not "a person who can be relied on to exercise proper stewardship of a publicly quoted company." Nevertheless, he continued to buy up newspapers and publishers and appeared both wealthy and successful. However, rumors spread that all was not well. He stifled public discussion by using libel lawyers to sue for damages, but his operations had long been financed by raiding the large pension funds of his companies.

Exposure

By 1990, Maxwell's operations were coming under closer scrutiny by the press, particularly those journals owned by his arch-rival, Rupert Murdoch. In May 1991 it was first alleged that Maxwell's companies were failing to provide information to meet company law. At the same time, groups of Maxwell employees alerted to what was happening to their pension funds, began to complain to the regulatory authorities in both the UK and US. Against a backdrop of rising interest rates and deepening recession, his

Above Robert Maxwell (inset) and the *Lady Ghislaine*, from which he was lost overboard.

businesses became increasingly exposed. Most of his borrowing had only been possible by using his holdings in Maxwell Communications and Mirror Group Newspapers as security with the banks. They had the right to sell these securities as economic conditions worsened, but as they did so, this depressed the value of his remaining shares and their value as security for other borrowings. Desperately, Maxwell began making even deeper inroads into company pension schemes and other assets to buy more shares to shore up their value as security for his debts. But the writing was all too clearly on the wall.

Fallout

On November 5, 1991, while cruising off the Canary Islands on his yacht the *Lady Ghislaine*, Maxwell was reported missing. He had last been seen on the upper deck and it was assumed he had fallen overboard. His body was later retrieved from the ocean and his funeral took place in Israel. There were many veiled references to his secret services on behalf of the Jewish state in earlier years. There were also suggestions that he might have been called upon to face war crime charges relating to an alleged shooting while he was an Army officer in Germany at the end of the war, and it was widely assumed that this, and the unravelling of his business empire, had caused him to commit suicide. However, there were persistent rumors that his shadowy role in intelligence matters had brought about his murder.

The Australian Wheat Board Scandal (2006)

Between the first Gulf War and the 2003 invasion of Iraq, the UN relaxed its embargo to allow the trading of oil for food to prevent starvation, which the Australian Wheat Board exploited through large-scale fraud.

Background

The Australian Wheat Board was a government body that bought wheat from Australian farmers to guarantee fair prices on world markets. On April 14, 1995, the United Nations, worried that sanctions on Saddam Hussein's regime were affecting vulnerable groups such as children, passed resolution 986. This allowed Iraq to sell a restricted amount of oil on world markets in exchange for food and medicine. In July 1999 the Australian Wheat Board was privatized as AWB Limited. Now owned by the wheat growers themselves, it moved quickly to ensure a leading role in supplying this new market.

Deception

Barred from using oil profits for more weapons, Saddam Hussein demanded bribes from companies joining the food-for-oil trade. Where US wheat growers had been shut out by sanctions, AWB had a golden opportunity. The Iraqis insisted on charging a fee of $12 on each ton of wheat supplied, for transportation costs—the transaction was handled through Alia, a Jordanian company with no transport vehicles at all. Since AWB's first order was for 600,000 tons of wheat, this added up to a huge bribe of $7.2 million. AWB decided to recoup the costs by sending inflated invoices to the UN for payment, and this arrangement ensured it soon became the largest supplier of food under the UN scheme, with payments and kickbacks rising steadily.

Exposure

With almost no monitoring of the contracts, AWB continued trading until the 2003 invasion. However when Baghdad fell in April, searches of government offices revealed details of the AWB deals to the Americans, whose own wheat growers had lost out as a direct result of AWB's bribes. At first, the Australian Department of Foreign Affairs and Trade, which had suspected the AWB of bribery over the oil-for-food program as far back as January 2000, tried to suggest that Alia might have paid the kickbacks to the regime without involving AWB at all. In 2005 the UN set up its own enquiry, which found that AWB had sold Iraq grain worth some $2.3 billion, on which it had paid $221 million in "transportation costs," making it the largest provider of funds to Saddam Hussein's regime. The Australian Government denied all knowledge of both deals and payments, though critics continue to insist this is extremely unlikely.

Fallout

In 2006, the Australian Government set up the Cole enquiry to investigate the scandal, in the wake of which AWB managing director Andrew Lindburg resigned. The enquiry exonerated both him and the government, but reported on November 24 that up to a dozen AWB officials may have committed crimes in running the fraud. It was left to the Federal Police to decide if further action should be taken. The US wheat growers, however, were not so accommodating, announcing in July 2006 that they would be pursuing a $1 billion damages claim against AWB, on the grounds that it had won a major share of the grain market using bribery and other corrupt activities.

The Litvinenko Murder (2006)

The sudden death of Russian emigré Alexander Litvinenko proved to be murder, with worrying overtones for East-West relations.

Background

Alexander Litvinenko was a former officer in the Soviet KGB (secret police) who had emigrated to the West and become an outspoken critic of the current Putin regime and its erosion of freedom in Russia. He claimed that the regime was involved in the unexplained deaths of other critics, which meant that he, too, was at risk from agents of the FSB, the successor to the KGB.

Deception

Litvinenko held material relating to the shooting of another dissident in Moscow, the investigative journalist Anna Politovskaya. This he had agreed to share with Mario Scaramella, an Italian academic. They met on November 11, 2006 in a London sushi bar called Itsu. Later the same day, he also met three fellow former agents of the KGB, Dmitri Kowtun, Andrei Lugovoi, and Vyacheslav Sokolenko, in the Pine Bar of the Millennium Hotel. After this meeting he returned to his home in Muswell Hill, but soon started to feel extremely ill. After three days with increasing stomach pains he was taken to two different hospitals, but his condition worsened.

Exposure

Three weeks later, Litvinenko was dead. Tests showed high levels of a toxic substance in his urine—Polonium 210, which emits high quantities of alpha particles and is deadly if ingested. The radiation trail was followed back from Litvinenko to both hospitals where he had been treated, to the sushi bar, the Millennium Hotel, and to the London offices of exiled Russian businessman

Boris Berezovsky. Traces were also found on two airliners that had made recent flights between Moscow and London. The implications were sinister. Though lethal if ingested, Polonium 210 is easily transported without danger, but can only be obtained by access to a working nuclear reactor. The evidence strongly suggested that this was a killing linked to government.

Fallout

This seemed to confirm Litvinenko's fears about being a potential FSB target. He had met the former KGB men on several occasions before November 11, including a meeting at the sushi bar. It would have been comparatively simple for one of them to lace the food or drink with polonium, and this would have tied in with the Russian intelligence services' tradition of eliminating opponents. The British Government requested Lugovoi's extradition from Russia to help with the investigation, but this was refused. Lugovoi has denied any involvement in Litvinenko's death, but the impasse has caused a chilling in relations between Britain and Russia.

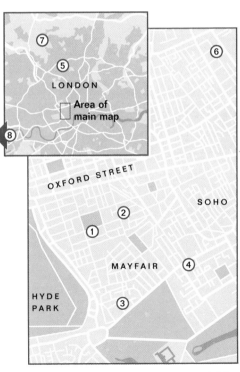

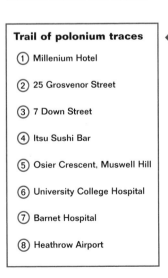

Trail of polonium traces

1. Millenium Hotel
2. 25 Grosvenor Street
3. 7 Down Street
4. Itsu Sushi Bar
5. Osier Crescent, Muswell Hill
6. University College Hospital
7. Barnet Hospital
8. Heathrow Airport

Part Four:
Political Scandals

Teapot Dome (1922)

Leases for the valuable oil reserves at Teapot Dome in Wyoming caused a notorious bribery scandal.

Background

Before the First World War, President Taft had reserved valuable oil fields on public land at Teapot Dome in Casper County, Wyoming, and at Elk Hills and Buena Vista Hills in California to supply the US Navy, then switching from coal to oil fuel for its warships. The decision created opposition from private oil interests, who claimed they could meet all the Navy's potential requirements. Later, a campaign to overturn the decision was led by Albert B. Fall, elected Republican Senator for New Mexico in 1912. Nine years on, Fall's supporters managed to persuade incoming President Warren G. Harding to appoint him Secretary of the Interior.

Deception

In 1922, Fall persuaded Secretary of the Navy, Edwin Denby, to transfer the oil fields to his own Interior Department, and an executive order was signed by President Harding. Fall then leased the Teapot Dome field to Harry F. Sinclair, of Sinclair Oil, without going through the normal competitive bidding process (not actually a legal requirement at the time.) The California oil fields he leased to Edward L. Doheny of Pan American Petroleum, again without a formal tender. The parties were careful to cover up the rest of the deal—Doheny's interest-free loan to Fall of $100,000 and gifts from both oilmen amounting to another $404,000, all of them strictly illegal. Furthermore, when Fall retired from his post the following year, Sinclair gave him another massive interest-free loan.

Exposure

On April 14, 1922 the *Wall Street Journal* revealed that Fall had transferred valuable oil leases without competitive tendering. Fall was unabashed, insisting he had done nothing illegal, and the matter would have rested but for the introduction of a Senate motion the next day to set up an official enquiry by the Public Lands Committee into the deal. Even then it seemed Fall was in the clear, but during the following two years the Montana Democrat Senator Thomas J. Walsh kept pressing him for more information. Two questions in particular would not go away. How did Fall account for the spectacular improvement in his lifestyle, and how did papers vital to the enquiry continue to disappear?

Fallout

Just as the enquiry was about to wind up, Walsh managed to find one vital piece of paper Fall had failed to destroy: A note referring to Doheny's loan of $100,000. It was enough. Congress ordered the President to declare the leases fraudulent and branded the decision transferring the oil fields to Fall's jurisdiction as illegal. In 1927, the US Supreme Court gave control of the oil fields back to the Navy and all three men involved were prosecuted. Two years later Fall was found guilty of bribery, fined $100,000 and jailed for a year. Sinclair was fined a similar amount and given a six-month sentence for threatening jury members and refusing to cooperate with the enquiry, while Doheny was acquitted. President Harding was exonerated but never recovered from the stress of the affair.

Cash for Honors (1922)

First World War British Premier
David Lloyd George made
worthwhile reforms but selling
honors to raise party funds
ended his political career.

Background

David Lloyd George was appointed Chancellor of the Exchequer in Asquith's
Liberal Government in 1908 at the age of 45. After the outbreak of war in
1914, he was appointed Minister for Munitions, where his energy and drive
helped eliminate bottlenecks in the supply of shells for every new attempt to
break the trench warfare deadlock. In 1916, the Liberals split into those who
wanted to retain power by a coalition with the Conservatives and those under
Asquith who refused. Lloyd George allied himself with the coalition wing of
the party and became a successful wartime prime minister.

Deception

It was already common for political parties to reward supporters with honors,
but discreetly to avoid alienating public opinion. Lloyd George found his party
starved of cash. He needed to raise funds quickly, so in December 1916 an
office was set up in Parliament Square, run by theatrical impresario Maundy
Gregory, and helped by Lloyd George's press agent and his Chief Whip. There
was a tariff for different honors, with a basic charge of £10,000 for a
knighthood, up to £40,000 for a baronetcy, and £50,000 plus for higher ranks
of the peerage. To avoid press scrutiny, the most powerful newspaper magnates
were given titles without any money having to change hands. By July 1922,
1,500 people had found the cash to buy a knighthood, and 91 peers had been
created, more than double the total of those ennobled since the beginning of
the century. The scheme brought some £2 million, a colossal sum for the times

into Lloyd George's hands. Gregory had even introduced the Order of the British Empire (OBE) as an honor that could be bought by those unwilling or unable to raise the cost of a knighthood, but this became suspect in the eyes of the public, who insisted the letters stood for the "Order of the Bad Egg."

Exposure

What eventually killed the arrangement was the controversy surrounding many of those who benefited from it. A Glasgow bookmaker, Richard Williamson, was found to have a criminal record after purchasing a Commander of the Order of the British Empire (CBE), and Sir Rowland Hodge, who had bought a baronetcy in 1921, had been found guilty of the criminal offense of food hoarding three years earlier. More and more people who knew nothing about the arrangement were complaining that those featured in the official Honors Lists seemed to be limited to wealthy newspaper owners and businessmen, and King George V was becoming increasingly unhappy at the scheme, occasionally refusing to grant honors bought by the most dubious characters. Matters finally came to a head with the publication of the 1922 Honors List. This included Joseph Robinson, recently convicted of a £0.5 million share fraud, William Vestey, convicted of tax evasion, and most notoriously of all, John Drughorn, who had been convicted of trading with the enemy while the war was at its height. It was too much for the King, who declared the list an insult to the Crown and the House of Lords. The press blew open the whole system to a shocked public.

Fallout

Lloyd George denied any responsibility for the sale of honors, and appointed a Royal Commission to look into the affair, after carefully limiting its powers to making future recommendations rather than investigating past errors. All the same, Parliament knew who to blame. The Conservatives withdrew their support from the coalition, Lloyd George resigned in October 1922, and never held political office again. The Commission's report resulted in the introduction of measures to ensure the sale of honors could never happen again, though this was far from the last time allegations would be made.

The Profumo Affair (1963)

The involvement of the UK War Minister with a woman who had links to the Soviet Naval Attaché nearly brought down the UK Conservative Government.

Background

John Profumo was heir to a Sardinian barony and a highly successful politician. Elected to Parliament in 1940 aged just 25, he reached the rank of Brigadier in his war service, and was reelected an MP in 1950. Serving as Secretary of State for War in the Conservative Government of Prime Minister Harold Macmillan in the early 1960s—and married to famous and successful actress Valerie Hobson—he seemed to have the brightest of futures. In 1961, he and his wife were invited to a house party at Cliveden, the Buckinghamshire stately home of Lord Astor, organized by a society osteopath and provider of girls for expensive parties named Stephen Ward. There he recognized a 19-year-old showgirl, Christine Keeler, apparently climbing naked out of the swimming pool after Ward had removed her costume. Profumo admitted later he had met Keeler previously at a London night club where she worked as a hostess—and where he had bought her a drink. He asked Ward for her phone number as she left with a Russian named Ivanov.

Deception

Profumo soon began an affair with Christine Keeler. The danger was that Ivanov was actually a Soviet naval officer, a senior attaché at the London embassy. Ward told MI5 (the UK's counter-intelligence and security agency) of the affair, who warned Profumo of the security implications, and he ended their relationship. Though there was never any direct evidence of a security threat, he had a great deal to lose if the affair ever became public. In December

1962, an incident involving Johnny Edgecombe, a West Indian who also had a sexual relationship with Keeler, fired a gun outside her flat which led to the press probing her background. When she failed to turn up to give evidence at his trial and fled to Spain, the story began to emerge, including her relationships with Profumo and Ivanov. At that stage the press kept quiet, but the final exposure followed on March 20, 1963, when opposition MPs George Wigg and Barbara Castle used the apparent security threat to air rumors that Profumo had had a sexual relationship with Keeler. Because of Parliamentary privilege, they could make these accusations without fear of a libel case and Profumo had serious questions to answer.

Above John Profumo, War Minister, who resigned after disclosure of his affair with Keeler.

Exposure

Profumo admitted two days later that he knew Christine Keeler, but denied there was anything improper in their relationship. But too many people were now aware of the reality and Stephen Ward, facing trial for living on immoral earnings as the Establishment closed ranks, wrote to the prime minister and Opposition Leader Harold Wilson to alert them to the truth. Finally, in the summer of 1963, Profumo took his wife to Venice to confess and returned to apologize on June 5, for having lied to the House of Commons. He resigned from the government, Parliament, and the Privy Council.

Fallout

John Profumo's constituents were furious at what they saw as the political hypocrisy of those who brought him down. Lord Denning's enquiry into the affair concluded there had been no real threat to security, while Stephen Ward committed suicide in August 1963 and Christine Keeler went to prison for nine months for perjury. Profumo himself went to work for the rest of his life as an unpaid volunteer at Toynbee Hall, a

charity based in London's East End, where he did everything from cleaning the toilets to raising funds. His wife joined him in his charity work until she died in 1998, and his public work and refusal to comment on the scandal finally resulted in the award of a Commander of the Order of the British Empire (CBE) in 1975. On March 9, 2006 at the age of 91, he died after a severe stroke and tributes poured in from those who knew him best.

Above Christine Keeler, the call girl involved with Lord John Profumo, was also sleeping with a Soviet spy trying to discover British nuclear secrets.

The Chappaquiddick Incident (1969)

Senator Edward Kennedy's Presidential hopes were dashed by his involvement in the death of one of his team after a road accident where he failed to summon help.

Background

After the deaths of both his older brothers Jack and Robert in political assassinations, Democrat Senator Edward Kennedy was widely expected to run for the Presidency in 1972. But in 1969 he went to a barbecue reunion for the Boiler Room Girls, a team of young political workers who worked on Robert Kennedy's 1968 campaign. The party was held on Friday, July 18 on Chappaquiddick Island, off the coast of Martha's Vineyard and connected by a small ferry. One of the girls, 22-year-old Mary Jo Kopechne, wanted to catch the ferry back to her hotel at Edgartown on Martha's Vineyard, and Kennedy offered her a lift. They left at 11:15 PM and headed for the ferry landing. But instead of turning left for the ferry, Kennedy turned right towards the beach where they had been swimming that afternoon, and found himself on the sharp bend leading to the narrow, ramshackle Dike Bridge with neither lights nor guardrails. Before he could slow down, the car veered off the bridge and turned over into the water. Kennedy himself managed to escape, but after seven or eight attempts to rescue Mary Jo, hampered by a strong running tide, he went for help.

Deception

Kennedy ran back to the cottage where the party had been held. He then returned to the bridge with two friends, Joe Gargan and Paul Markham, who dived into the water, but had no more success at reaching the trapped girl.

Above A tow truck pulls Senator Edward Kennedy's car out of Poucha Pond after the Senator's infamous accident on Chappaquiddick Island.

Although they passed a local fire station, and there was a payphone near the bridge, no one apparently thought to call for help. Finally, they decided the aides would tell the other party guests while Kennedy dealt with the accident. Then, in spite of all that happened, he went into a phase of apparent denial, returned to his hotel room, and went to sleep.

Exposure

After waking up on the Saturday morning, the Senator called his legal team. By that time, local fishermen had spotted the upturned car. By the time Kennedy called at the local Edgartown police station at 10:00 AM, Mary Jo's body had been recovered. He made a brief written statement, omitting the repeated rescue attempts, and blurring the delay of ten hours between the accident and his visit to the police station.

Fallout

By the time the story was out, the other party guests had left the island, but a local sheriff's deputy reported seeing a car like Kennedy's, with a similar license plate number and a man and a woman inside, sitting at the junction between the ferry and the bridge, a full hour and a half after the reported time of the accident. This has never been properly explained and conflicts with Kennedy's version of events, thereby generating a whole series of conspiracy theories—one of the most persistent of these being a suggestion that Mary Jo had taken Kennedy's car on her own, for whatever reason, had missed the turn off for the ferry, and had driven off the bridge in confusion.

For his part, Kennedy resolutely denied he had been drinking or that there had been any immoral conduct between himself and Mary Jo. The local medical examiner confirmed she had died from drowning and her body was taken back to her parents' home in Pennsylvania, where Kennedy attended her funeral four days later. On July 25 he appeared in court to plead guilty to a charge of leaving an accident and was given a two-month suspended sentence. But he faced an uncertain political future. Local voters strongly supported him as did his Senate colleagues, but his Presidential prospects suffered the greatest damage, particularly after the inquest concluded his negligence had contributed to Mary Jo's death.

Kennedy declined to run for the Presidency in 1972, a decision he repeated in 1976. But his solid committee work over the ensuing years built him a high political reputation as a genuine liberal, who could persuade opponents and support allies to the greatest effect. As one of his last acts before his death in the summer of 2009, he gave his full endorsement to the candidacy of Barack Obama, which helped to ensure the election of America's first-ever African-American President.

Willy Brandt's Spy Secretary (1974)

East German espionage efforts led to the political downfall of West German Chancellor Willy Brandt, a strong supporter of rapprochement with the East, which they later admitted was one of their worst mistakes.

Background

The popular West German politician Willy Brandt was born in 1913 as Herbert Ernst Karl Frahm. In 1933 he fled Nazi oppression as radicals were sent to the newly opened concentration camps. In Norway he adopted the name of Willy Brandt to confuse pursuers and was eventually granted Norwegian nationality. He returned to Germany after the war and in 1948, under his new name, became a German citizen once more and reentered politics. He became Mayor of West Berlin in 1957, where he won a world-wide reputation following a series of challenges from Russia and East Germany. Finally, at his third attempt in 1969, he was elected West German Chancellor. This allowed him to develop a much more conciliatory policy towards the East, while maintaining his vigorous defence of Western values shown during his days in Berlin. In 1970, *Time* magazine named him Man of the Year, and in 1971 he was awarded the Nobel Peace Prize for his role in bringing East and West Germany closer together.

Deception

His policy caused much controversy within Germany, and opponents accused him of over-friendliness with the still overtly hostile and suspicious East German regime. Their espionage service scored a great coup when in the early 1970s they managed to place one of their undercover agents, Günther

Guillaume, as an assistant in Brandt's office. Yet it was also already clear they valued Brandt's contribution to easing East-West tension. When opposition politicians forced a vote of no confidence on April 27, 1972 which could have deposed him as Chancellor, the two vital votes which saved him were cast by two opposition members, bribed by the East German Stasi secret police to vote to keep Brandt in office.

Exposure
Guillaume and his wife arrived as refugees from the East in 1956, but had already been recruited as agents by the Stasi. By 1973, Guillaume's role was leaked to the West German security service. They told Brandt, but asked him to continue working with Guillaume as usual. Finally, on April 24, 1974 Guillaume was arrested and the truth revealed. The government accused Brandt of complicity and he resigned as Chancellor, exactly the result the East Germans hoped to avoid.

Fallout
In later years, Brandt revealed the scandal had broken at a time when he had been wanting to stand down because of mounting problems with alcohol, depression, and an overactive private life, compounded with the political challenges of coping with the economic fallout from the 1973 hike in worldwide oil prices. He was succeeded as Chancellor by Helmut Schmidt but he remained in politics, serving in the European Parliament from 1979 to 1983, and was a strong supporter of Germany's eventual reunification. Guillaume was sentenced to 13 years in jail but was released in exchange for Western agents in 1981. He was feted as a hero in the East, became a trainer of spies, and after reunification he was given immunity from further prosecution.

Cash for Questions (1994)

Scandals exposing MPs' greed
have damaged both main UK
political parties in
successive administrations.

Background

Members of Parliament (MPs) frequently ask questions in the House on
matters raised by constituents or subjects of public interest, but it is illegal
for them to charge for doing so. In October 1994, *The Guardian* newspaper
alleged that lobbyist Ian Greer had effectively bribed two Conservative MPs,
Tim Smith and Neil Hamilton, to ask Parliamentary questions on behalf of
Mohammed Fayed, owner of Harrods department store. The paper stated that
Fayed himself had originally accused Greer of paying the MPs to table questions
on his behalf for £2,000 per question. All three denied the transactions. Tim
Smith insisted Greer had paid him nothing, but that Fayed had paid him
directly to raise questions on his behalf. Hamilton and Greer issued High
Court libel writs against *The Guardian*, but Conservative Prime Minister
John Major decided to set up the Nolan Committee, to be responsible for
maintaining standards of Parliamentary behavior.

Deception

In December 1994, Fayed claimed he had also paid Neil Hamilton directly
for Parliamentary questions on his behalf. In September 1996, when the libel
case was about to reach the courts, Fayed suddenly produced three members
of his staff who claimed to have processed payments to both men. Three days
later, both men withdrew the libel action. By now, the affair smacked of a
vendetta by Fayed against the individuals, or the government to which they
belonged. Nevertheless, their conduct appeared indefensible, and *The
Guardian* led a massive campaign of condemnation. Ian Greer's lobbying
company collapsed within three months.

Exposure

John Major commissioned an enquiry from senior civil servant Sir Gordon Downey. Major lost the 1997 election, partly as a result of the fall in public support resulting from the scandal. Tim Smith resigned as an MP, while Hamilton was opposed by former BBC reporter Martin Bell, standing as a self-styled "anti-corruption" candidate (habitually wearing a white suit to reemphasize his purity) but with massive help from the opposition parties. He was elected MP for Knutsford, the seat previously held by Hamilton.

Fallout

Two months after the election, the Downey enquiry cleared all three men of *The Guardian*'s original allegations. He admitted the claims of Fayed's staff about payments to Hamilton amounted to "compelling evidence," though he did not support their claims about payments to Greer. Three other MPs and former MPs alleged to have accepted Fayed payments were criticized. Neil Hamilton lost a libel case brought against Fayed in 1999 for more allegations made on TV. It was then discovered that privileged legal papers stolen from Hamilton's barristers were found in Fayed's possession. Though this implied misconduct by the other side in the case, Hamilton's resulting appeal was nevertheless dismissed and he was declared bankrupt in 2001. Since then the subsequent Labour Government has itself suffered a whole series of financial scandals, most recently the 2009 cash for questions allegations, where three Labour life peers, Lord Truscott, Lord Taylor of Blackburn, Lord Moonie, and Lord Snape discussed payment for amending laws with journalists posing as lobbyists. Police finally decided not to proceed with a criminal investigation. Fayed went on to lose his other legal campaign, to prove his son Dodi and the Princess of Wales had been murdered by an Establishment plot masterminded by the Duke of Edinburgh.

Impeach the President (1998)

Bill Clinton's Presidency
was dogged by allegations of
misconduct, most notoriously
with Monica Lewinsky, a
young White House intern.

Background

Bill Clinton was elected 42nd President in 1993, aged 46, and the third youngest to take office. But his reputation was tarnished by persistent rumors of sexual impropriety. While he was serving as Governor of Arkansas in 1991, one of his staff, 25-year-old Paula Jones, complained he had used State Police troopers to act as go-betweens to proposition her. In 1994, she sued him for $0.75 million for sexual harassment. Clinton challenged the case all the way to the Supreme Court, but eventually paid her a total of $850,000 in an out-of-court settlement. The court then ordered him to pay an additional $91,000 to compensate for damage caused by what it described as his false and misleading answers. But her legal team's search for other potential witnesses turned up much more damaging information.

Deception

In 1995 22-year-old Monica Lewinsky was appointed as an intern at the White House. Later that year, she and Clinton began a sexual relationship, and she claimed they had had sex in different parts of the White House on nine occasions between November 1995 and March 1997. In April 1996, as staff became aware of their involvement, she was reassigned to the Pentagon. There she confided her feelings to fellow worker Linda Tripp, who recorded their conversations. In January 1998, Lewinsky revealed she had been questioned by Paula Jones' lawyers but had denied any relationship with the President. This persuaded Linda Tripp to pass on her information to

Above Monica Lewinsky meeting President Bill Clinton at a White House function.

Kenneth Starr, the lawyer investigating Clinton on other sensitive matters.

Exposure

When challenged by Starr, the President denied any sexual relationship with Monica Lewinsky, until confronted by DNA evidence. This was found on a blue dress he had given Monica and which she had worn at the time of one of their liaisons. Linda Tripp had advised her to keep the dress as potential evidence without its being washed or dry-cleaned. His defense to accusations of perjury was that he did not define oral sex as sexual relations, although he later owned up to an inappropriate relationship. These statements did little to deflect growing political pressure for his impeachment. Finally, on December 19, 1998, the President was impeached by the House of Representatives on the specific charges of perjury and obstruction of justice. With his opponents in the Republican Party possessing a majority, it seemed he was doomed, but the final vote found him not guilty on both charges.

Fallout

This appeared as a case of the political classes protecting one of their own, and created a great deal of public criticism. Clinton was only the second American President to be impeached after Andrew Johnson. But public support revived, and when Bill Clinton finally left office at the end of his second term in 2001, he scored approval ratings of 66 percent, the highest of any President leaving office since the Second World War.

The Berlusconi Years (2009)

Italian Prime Minister Silvio Berlusconi has faced increasing criticism and allegations of bizarre behavior and involvement with young women, but he remains popular in his home country.

Background

Berlusconi has been a musician, singer and songwriter, cruise ship entertainer, property developer, businessman, media magnate, and politician, owner of the successful football team AC Milan, and is said to be the richest man in Italy. In 1994, he founded the center-right political party Forza Italia and three months later was elected to Parliament and appointed prime minister. However, persistent rumors of links with the Mafia and accusations of using his overwhelming domination of the Italian media to damage his enemies politically and economically have been thrown at him, though without any apparent damage to his voter appeal. His private life has earned him an equally threadbare reputation. In 1985 he divorced his first wife, Carla Elvira Dall'Oglo, with whom he had a son and daughter, to take up with actress Veronica Lario. They finally married in 1990 and had three more children. Berlusconi seems to survive and thrive in spite of the barrage of accusations directed at him. Voted out of office in 1995, he was reelected as prime minister in 2001, and served for five years—a long time in Italy's turbulent political system.

Deception

After losing office again in 2006, Berlusconi saw a further chance to regain power in 2008 when his principal opponent, Romano Prodi, had to call a

Above Berlusconi is accused of propositioning his self-appointed Equal Opportunities Minister, Mara Carfagna (top) and of having an affair with 18 year old Noemi Letizia (bottom).

snap election. The election saw Berlusconi returned to office once more, but was backed by more persistent rumors of scandals involving young women helping in his campaign, and centered on parties for supporters held at his house in Rome and his 300-acre Villa Certosa estate on the island of Sardinia.

Exposure

This time accusations came from within Berlusconi's own family. When he was quoted in January 2007 as having told one of his party's representatives, Mara Carfagna (a former showgirl appointed Equal Opportunities Minister in his administration) that he would marry her if he was free to do so, his wife demanded a public apology. Three months later she published an open letter criticizing his policy of selecting attractive young women with little or no political backing or experience as his party's candidates for the 2009 European elections. Berlusconi demanded an apology in turn for what he described as interference with his political campaign, and cast doubt on the future of the marriage. Days later he attended the 18th birthday party of Noemi Letizia, a girl who claimed she saw him as a father figure, and his wife filed divorce papers.

Fallout

From then on, new revelations appeared in quick succession. On May 24, 2009, Letizia's former boyfriend confirmed the girl had spent a week at Berlusconi's Sardinian villa over the New Year. On June 17, 2009 a retired actress, Patrizia D'Addario, working as an escort, claimed to have been paid to attend two of Berlusconi's parties, after one of which she spent the night with him. Tapes of their encounter later appeared in a left-wing paper. Allegations of payment for her services, from jewelry and cash in plain envelopes to help in restarting a stalled property development project, raised the possibility of prostitution charges. But as in all else, Berlusconi continues to protest his innocence—so far successfully.

MPs Expenses Scandal (2009)

Public trust in the UK political system was wrecked by leaked details of MPs' expenses claims and their strenuous efforts to prevent them being released.

Background

British Members of Parliament (MPs) can claim back expenses "wholly, exclusively, and necessarily" incurred in carrying out their duties, including maintaining a second home when they live far enough away from either their constituency or Parliament. In the wake of public anger at the spectacle of MPs voting themselves substantial pay rises, a culture arose whereby they treated the expenses allowances as a hidden but legitimate subsidy to increase their incomes without voter ire.

Deception

Normally the claims were kept secret, and only occasional leaks revealed the level of public money involved. Several MPs employed family members and outside staff unrelated to their duties. Others used second-home allowances to make large sums of money by carefully playing the property market. However, requests for details to be released under the 2000 Freedom of Information Act were refused and Parliament tried unsuccessfully to have expenses officially exempted from the Act. In February 2008, an Information Tribunal allowed a request under the Act for expenses claims to be made public. The House of Commons Authorities claimed this would be unduly intrusive, but in May 2008 the High Court decided the information was in the public interest, and the House of Commons promised to release some of the details in July 2009. They were preempted by a leaked copy of the expenses records, published in the *Daily Telegraph* on May 8, 2009.

Exposure

The revelations caused enormous national anger at the spectacle of a privileged class of nominally public servants enriching themselves at the expense of the taxpayer, especially at a time of economic recession. Some MPs had claimed for a second home under the rules when already enjoying an official residence provided by the taxpayer. Others repeatedly switched the designations of their main and second homes to avoid paying capital gains tax or stamp duty when selling a property, or used expenses to fund renovations of their main home to boost its market value. Some evaded paying income tax on benefits in kind, or had claimed for the services of an accountant to advise on their tax claims, both of which were strictly against the rules. Because receipts were not required for sums of less than £250, many items could not be checked. A food allowance of £400 per month without receipts, for example, was meant to help with additional costs while Parliament was sitting, but several MPs successfully claimed it through the long recesses as well. As the revelations inspired ever greater public fury, with one MP claiming for having the moat to his stately home cleaned and another repaid for a floating house to protect the ducks on his lake from predators), leaders of the three main political parties moved quickly to disown the members of their parties who had been responsible for the most extravagant claims. They promised tougher action in future to stamp out these abuses.

Fallout

After the revelations, many MPs and ministers attempted to retrieve their reputations by repaying some of the claims, or even by resigning from office. Others were threatened with expulsion by their parties, or deselection by their constituents. High profile casualties included no less than six government ministers, including Justice Minister Shahid Malik, Home Secretary Jacqui Smith, and Communities Secretary Hazel Blears. But the most spectacular resignation was that of Michael Martin, the Speaker of the House of Commons. He had been repeatedly criticized for failing to be sufficiently impartial in calling Members to speak in the House regarding the scandal, and for claiming large sums of money for taxis for his wife's shopping trips. When he concentrated his anger on those who had leaked expenses information

Above Hazel Blears MP and her husband Michael Halsall leave Salford Civic center where she survived a no confidence motion at a meeting of her constituency party on June 18, 2009.

rather than those MPs with such outrageous claims he was seen as a symbol of the now discredited culture that governed Parliamentary expenses, and was forced to step down. With a general election due before autumn 2010, many other MPs may well fall victim to public discontent. It is possible that one outcome of the scandal may be that increasing numbers of independent MPs end up in Parliament.

Part Five:
Military
Scandals

L'Affaire Dreyfus (1894)

Captain Alfred Dreyfus, a promising French Army officer, was convicted as a German spy on the flimsiest evidence and sentenced to life imprisonment on Devil's Island.

Background

Alfred Dreyfus came from a wealthy Jewish background and had won a place on the French Army General Staff. He had been born in Mulhouse in Alsace, a province annexed by the Germans after the Franco-Prussian War of 1871, where his father still lived. In October 1894, Captain Dreyfus was charged with passing French military secrets to the Germans. Two months, later a military tribunal sentenced him to solitary confinement for life in the terrible conditions of Devil's Island off the coast of French Guiana.

Deception

The evidence centered on a handwritten list found by a French cleaner in the wastepaper basket of the German military attaché at the Paris embassy, offering to supply French military secrets. Dreyfus was suspected due to his links with German territory, and also because he was a Jew, in an army where anti-Semitism was still common. The investigators searched everywhere for corroborative evidence. They found none, but continued with the case. When forensic experts rejected the suggestion that the list was in Dreyfus's handwriting, this was too much for a Lt. Col Henry, who paid a forger called Lemercier-Picard to produce a letter from the Italian military attaché to his German opposite number, naming Dreyfus as the spy.

Exposure

In spite of the lies and false evidence, the public began to realize something was seriously wrong with the whole affair. On January 13, 1898 the eminent writer Émile Zola wrote an open letter to President Faure, which was published in the newspaper *L'Aurore* under the title "J'Accuse" ("I accuse"). The article alleged that the government had shown anti-Semitism in what it described as the unlawful imprisonment of Alfred Dreyfus. Zola was prosecuted for libel and had to flee to England until the furor died down. In the meantime, a Dreyfus supporter, Lt. Col Georges Picquart, pointed out the resemblance between the writing of the original document and a later letter from Major Ferdinand Esterhazy, who had served with several of those involved in convicting Dreyfus in French Army counterintelligence. Picquart was posted to Tunisia to remove him from the scene. In the meantime, Henry removed some of the papers from the dossier of false evidence against Dreyfus, unaware that Picquart had had them photographed. When the tampering and forgery were discovered, Henry was arrested and days later cut his own throat in prison. These revelations resulted in the Court of Cassation ordering a new trial in 1899 where, astonishingly, Dreyfus was reconvicted and sentenced to another 10 years in jail, such was the opposition at the highest level to his release.

Fallout

Dreyfus had to wait until July 1906 for a Presidential pardon and the reversal of his conviction, when he was promoted to Major and awarded the *Légion d'Honneur*. He retired from the army a year later but was recalled in 1914, serving at Verdun and at the Chemin des Dames. He retired for a second time in 1919 as a Lieutenant Colonel, and died on July 12, 1935 at the age of 76.

The Tonkin Gulf Incident (1964)

A skirmish off the coast of North Vietnam between US Navy warships and
North Vietnamese patrol boats provided the perfect cover for President Lyndon Johnson to send American help to the region.

Background
The 1954 Geneva Conference effectively split Vietnam (until then part of French Indo-China) into the Communist North Vietnam and the anti-Communist South Vietnam. By 1961, North Vietnam was backing an insurrection in the south with a view to reunifying the country under Communist control. This led President John F. Kennedy to send in US advisors to help the South Vietnamese contain the rebellion. Following Kennedy's assassination in November 1963, his successor Lyndon Johnson became President. Johnson wanted to switch to a more direct military involvement to stop what he believed was a consequence of Soviet-backed expansion in the region.

Deception
What Johnson needed to carry political and public opinion with him was a direct threat to US interests, so that he could introduce new legislation allowing him to commit American forces in Vietnam without either a declaration of war or the backing of Congress. During the summer of 1964, Norwegian-built patrol boats crewed by South Vietnamese sailors were operating under US orders on raids against two islands off the North Vietnamese coast. On July 31, the destroyer USS *Maddox* was also in the area, carrying out an electronic warfare mission in support of the raids but under orders not to approach closer than eight miles to the coast or four

miles to the nearer of the two islands. On August 2, it was 28 miles (45 km) offshore when it reported being attacked by three North Vietnamese patrol boats, which it drove off with fire from its five-inch guns. The only damage to the destroyer was a hit by a single round from a heavy machine gun. Two days later, the *Maddox* returned on another electronic intelligence-gathering mission with a second destroyer, the USS *Turner Joy*. Both ships reported being attacked by North Vietnamese boats, which fired torpedoes at them but missed.

Exposure

It later emerged the second attack never really happened. Within hours, the commander of the *Maddox*, Captain John J. Herrick, signaled Washington twice to report that freak radar and sonar conditions led to a fairly chaotic situation with false echoes, which suggested weapons had been fired when in fact no actual attack had been launched. Even the first attack on his ship on August 2, was a great deal less threatening than reported. An internal study by the US National Security Agency released in 2005 revealed that when the *Maddox* was approached by the first three North Vietnamese patrol boats, it fired a series of three warning shots from its five-inch main armament, whereupon the boats retreated at high speed without delivering any return fire. At the time, however, the Johnson administration insisted the US warships had come under fire from the North Vietnamese craft on both occasions.

Above Map showing the Gulf of Tonkin where the alleged incident took place.

Fallout

The immediate result of the Tonkin Gulf Incident was that the President was able to claim that US warships had been attacked in international waters without provocation. He broadcast to the nation on August 4, and ordered air attacks against North Vietnam. Strike aircraft from the carriers USS *Ticonderoga* and USS *Constellation*, also in the Gulf of Tonkin area, hit the bases for the torpedo boats and their refueling facilities in Operation Pierce Arrow. On August 7, just five days after the claimed initial attack on the *Maddox*, Congress passed the Southeast Asia Resolution, granting the President the right to assist any country in the region under threat from Communist aggression without a formal declaration of war, and without Senate approval. This gave Johnson the authority he needed to move massive US forces into South Vietnam, though much later he admitted the decision had been based on an attack that never really happened. The ultimate result of the Tonkin Gulf incident was a long and divisive war that America ultimately lost, and which split the nation as never before, spawning a much deeper distrust of political leaders.

Above The Aircraft carrier USS *Constellation* was used in the first strikes against North Vietnam.

Massacre at My Lai (1968)

During the Vietnam War, a US unit massacred inhabitants of a village they believed had been harboring the enemy.

Background

In January 1968, the North Vietnamese Tet Offensive attacked deep into US-held territory in South Vietnam using units that then hid among the population. A company of the US 20th Infantry Division (1st battalion, Charlie Company), which had five men killed and many more wounded from mines and booby traps, was sent in on March 16 to follow up an intelligence report that the unit responsible for their losses, the North Vietnamese 48th Battalion, was being sheltered by the inhabitants of My Lai. They were given an aggressive briefing by senior officers who insisted all the loyal villagers would have left for the markets by 7:00 AM and that anyone left must be supporting the North Vietnamese. They were ordered to kill any guerrillas hiding in the villages, together with any "suspects," and then to slaughter livestock, poison wells, and burn down houses.

What began as a dismal task soon turned into a blood bath. No enemy soldiers were found in the village, but the troops were convinced they might be hiding beneath the houses of relatives or supporters, and began shooting at "suspected enemy positions." This quickly degenerated into indiscriminate slaughter, as villagers including children and babies were killed with gunfire, bayonets, and grenades. Women were raped, and the operation only stopped when everyone at the scene was dead. The Americans had suffered one man killed and seven wounded from mines and booby traps in the area, but between 350 and 500 unarmed Vietnamese civilians had died.

Deception

News of the massacre only leaked out months later. At the time a US Army helicopter pilot, Warrant Officer Hugh Thompson, had flown over the village and been appalled at what he had seen happening below. He landed nearby and tried to help the villagers, radioing for help to treat the wounded, but ground troops continued with the killing. Thompson took off and landed a second time where civilians were being approached by ground troops. This time he told his crewmen that if the ground troops started killing the Vietnamese, they were to open fire on the US soldiers, and he managed to ensure the civilians were flown out to safety. Nevertheless, the first official report of the one-sided slaughter claimed 128 Viet Cong, 22 civilians had been killed during a fierce fire fight, and the American commander, General William Westmoreland, congratulated the unit on the outstanding job they had done.

Above Civilian women and children rounded up to be killed by US army, during pursuit of Viet Cong militia.

Exposure

Colonel Henderson of the 11th Light Infantry Brigade was ordered to interview several of the soldiers involved, and in late April 1968 his report claimed 20 civilians had died during the operation. In October, a GI belonging to the brigade, Tom Glen, wrote to Westmoreland's replacement as US commander complaining that brutality towards Vietnamese was routine and widespread. But the lid was only finally lifted when Ron Ridenhour, a former member of Charlie Company who had not been present on the day, wrote to President Nixon and other public figures in March 1969 revealing what had happened.

Fallout

It still took another eight months before all the details were released. Widespread public revulsion caused a steep drop in support for the war and the army conducted its own investigation into the killings. Though senior officers were criticized for covering up the atrocity, only a handful were charged with misconduct. One was Colonel Henderson, later acquitted; another, Captain Medina, commander of Charlie Company who denied ordering the massacre, was also acquitted. The third was Lieutenant William Calley, charged with premeditated murder for ordering his men to open fire on civilians. On March 29, 1971, Calley was sentenced to life imprisonment, but after President Nixon released him pending his appeal, he only served six weeks in the military prison at Fort Benning, Georgia.

Operation Menu (1969)

Cambodian neutrality in the
Vietnam War enabled the Army of
North Vietnam and the Viet Cong
irregulars to use the country
for refuge, supplies, and training areas,
so the Nixon administration ordered secret
bombing raids against these targets.

Background

President Nixon was firmly convinced that Cambodia's ruler, Sihanouk, was allowing North Vietnamese units to rest and resupply in Cambodian territory, and was determined to prevent enemy soldiers remaining out of reach of US retaliation. Invading a nominally neutral country was politically dangerous, so a clandestine bombing campaign was launched instead. The final trigger was the launching of the Tet Offensive in January 1969 by the North Vietnamese deep into US-held territory. Even though Sihanouk had become closer to the Americans by then, it was decided to open the bombing campaign on the night of March 18, 1969 with a force of 60 B52 heavy bombers. The main target was the supposed site of the Communist forces' headquarters in an area of Cambodia called the Fishhook, though the bomber crews were briefed that they were attacking Vietnamese territory. A total of 2,400 tons of bombs were dropped on Cambodia. The campaign continued for 14 months, directed against five more base areas, involving the dropping of more than 108,000 tons of bombs.

Deception

None of this was allowed to leak to the outside world. Each operation was planned and ordered by a team of the most senior Navy and Air Force officers and politicians, and its nature was concealed by publicity that raids were being directed at targets in Vietnam but close to the Cambodian border. An officer within the screen of secrecy was responsible for setting the coordinates on the radar-controlled Skyspot guidance system, which relayed computer-generated target data to the approaching bombers. Aboard the aircraft, the only crew members who really knew the nature of their targets were the pilots and navigators; everyone else was told the bombers were over Vietnamese territory. After the completion of each mission, all the paperwork and computer records were destroyed.

Exposure

Neither Sihanouk nor the North Vietnamese released any information on the air attacks. An article had appeared in the *New York Times* in May 1969 claiming that Cambodia was being bombed and citing an anonymous source within the Nixon administration. The FBI was called in, and suspected an aide in the office of Henry Kissinger. The first of numerous President-authorized phone taps was set up to monitor his communications, but without result. Only in December 1972 did the full truth emerge, after Major Knight, operator of the Skyspot bombing guidance system for the B52s, had been discharged from the Air Force following complaints he had made to his seniors over the legality of their actions. He finally wrote to Senator William Proxmire, who referred it to the Senate Armed Services Committee, which was powerful enough to demand the Defense Department release all records relating to the Cambodia bombing.

Fallout

The depth and cynicism of the cover-up caused a steeper fall in public support for the war, and for the President. In Cambodia itself it brought about the fall of Prince Sihanouk and the rise of the Khmer Rouge rebels who would eventually seize power and bring about the deaths of millions in the so-called "Killing Fields." Perhaps the most surprising revelation came in 2000 when President Clinton ordered the release of information on all American bombing over Indo-China. This showed that raids on Cambodia had begun as far back as 1965 under the Johnson Presidency, with more than 2.7 million tons of bombs being dropped on Cambodian territory, which meant that the raids from 1969 to 1970 were a small fraction of an equally secretive but much larger 11-year campaign.

Weapons of Mass Destruction (2003)

A prime reason for invading Iraq in 2003 was the threat of weapons of mass destruction (WMD), but the threat was founded on a false premise.

Background

In the years when Saddam Hussein ruled Iraq, he was known to have developed biological and nuclear weapons. He used chemical weapons against his own people as well as enemy forces in the Iran–Iraq War. One of the consequences of his invasion of Kuwait on August 2, 1990 and his defeat in the 1990–91 Gulf War was that he had to ensure his weapons stocks were destroyed and allow regular United Nations inspections to prove no new stocks were being built up. Gradually Iraqi cooperation with UN inspectors diminished in mutual hostility, and the inspectors were withdrawn in 1998. They were only sent back to Iraq in November 2002 after a new UN resolution demanded complete co-operation with the inspection system.

Deception

What followed was an extraordinary double deception. The Americans and the British were clearly so publicly convinced that Saddam Hussein still had secret WMD stockpiles they used it as a reason to escalate the pressure towards an invasion. Saddam Hussein, on the other hand, was carrying out a delicate balancing act. Not wanting or believing that his enemies would actually attack, he clearly felt he could not reveal to friends and enemies alike that he no longer had any meaningful WMD reserves. This would leave him largely defenceless against other regional powers, and might even weaken his position in his own country. By March 2003, no one was happy with the

Above Map showing suspected Iraqi WMD facilities. These included uranium mines, nuclear research facilities, and weapon development centers.

situation. Hans Blix, chief of the UN inspection team, said Iraqi foot-dragging would mean it could take months to resolve whether any WMDs existed in Iraqi hands. The British and Americans, convinced the UN was being fooled by Saddam's delaying tactics, increased the pressure on the UN to support an invasion. To buttress their campaign, they claimed their intelligence sources clearly revealed large reserves of WMDs in Iraq.

Exposure

Following the invasion and the toppling of Saddam, an anxious search for evidence of the WMDs followed. Now at last there was noone who could bar access to sensitive sites or deny information to UN inspectors. Yet the results were overwhelmingly barren. No current weapons stockpiles were found, except for old chemical agent shells left over from the Iran–Iraq war. Experts testified that the limited shelf life of most WMDs meant old stocks would be worse than useless. In the UK, press revelations of government attempts to persuade the intelligence services to paint a more positive picture of the WMD threat and the subsequent death of Dr. David Kelly, a weapons expert criticized for speaking out of turn to the BBC and the wider media caused furious controversy. It became increasingly clear that the terrible costs of going to war had been incurred on what amounted to a false premise.

Fallout

Other uncomfortable facts emerged from the analysis that followed. It became increasingly clear that several nations had benefited greatly from supplying the facilities that allowed Saddam to build up his original stockpiles. France had built and equipped a nuclear reactor which eventually could have been used to produce weapons material, a threat so potent that it was destroyed by an Israeli airstrike, and the French were responsible for a fifth of Iraqi chemical weapons equipment. Ironically, the UK provided equipment for manufacturing mustard gas, and the US supplied biological warfare agents as part of a program intended to develop vaccines. But the most lasting legacy of the WMDs is that there has been a huge increase in violence and terrorism all over the world, which may eventually cost more lives than such weapons ever did.

Use of Torture (2005)

Widespread anger in the US at what was seen as a failure by the Central Intelligence Agency (CIA) to uncover details of the Al Qaeda plot to bring down the Twin Towers in time to prevent this, persuaded the Agency to introduce "enhanced interrogation" techniques to persuade future terrorist suspects to reveal vital information.

Background

In mid-March 2002, the controllers of the CIA decided that, in order to produce useful intelligence sensitive information from terrorist suspects quickly enough for effective action to be taken, tougher methods were required to persuade them to reveal what they knew. A range of physical techniques was specifically laid down, from slaps and punches to sleep deprivation and "waterboarding," to be used on top-level Al Qaeda suspects under closely-monitored conditions. Following the transfer of prisoners taken during the subsequent fighting in Iraq and Afghanistan to military detention at Guantanamo Bay, similar allegations were made of harsh treatment being used during interrogations.

Deception

As with "extraordinary rendition" (see page 136), details were shrouded in secrecy. Only a small group of CIA agents were involved, and they were limited to specific procedures laid down in internal documents. They could start with the "attention grab" by grasping the front of the suspect's clothing and giving a violent shaking. A sharp slap across the face would cause pain and trigger a climate of fear, but a slap to the belly had to be done with an open hand, as a clenched fist might cause internal damage. Prisoners could be forced to strip and stand, soaking wet, in cold cells, or sleep deprived, when the suspect was handcuffed and shackled with leg irons to a bolt in the floor and forced to stand in the same position for 48 hours or more. Most effective of all was "waterboarding," where the suspect would be strapped to a board, with his feet higher than his head. When a plastic sheet was placed over his face and water poured over it, this created an appalling sensation of drowning which forced almost instant cooperation with the interrogators.

Exposure

Lifting the cloak of secrecy began within the CIA itself. Officers were unhappy with official backing for what they felt was illegal mistreatment. They disliked the need for secrecy, because they felt this made them conspirators in a

Above An American soldier stands guard outside the controversial Abu Ghraib prison.

campaign to mislead the public, in the light of repeated official denials that the CIA imposed any pressure on suspects. Several officers insisted that information produced under this kind of pressure was often useless, because suspects would say anything they felt their interrogators wanted to hear. One suspect told his questioners that the Iraqis had trained Al Qaeda in biochemical weapons, and this influenced US policy during and after the invasion. It was later revealed he had no specialist knowledge at all, but his admission caused the ill-treatment to stop. When details of these concerns were finally revealed in late 2005, they caused a furious public outcry. In addition, a series of similar scandals relating to mistreatment of Iraqi prisoners by US and British forces followed the successful 2003 invasion. Allegations of torture, abuse, and threats at the American administered jail at Abu Ghraib near Baghdad resulted in charges being brought against military personnel. In September 2003, prisoner Baha Mousa died in British military custody in Basra, having suffered 93 separate wounds. Seven members of the Queen's Lancashire Regiment were later charged with war crimes. A total of almost £3 million was paid to the dependants of Baha Mousa and nine other prisoners in July 2008 for substantial breaches of their human rights. More recently, in November 2009, new allegations have been made including 33 cases of abuse and assault by British troops dating back to 2003, in what has been called "the British Abu Ghraib." These are currently being investigated by officials from the Ministry of Defence.

Fallout

President Obama acted quickly to stop these enhanced interrogation techniques when he took over as president in 2009. However, he enraged many of his supporters by refusing to release full details of individual cases, or to prosecute those who had carried out the interrogations under the 2002 policy. In addition, the planned trial of Khalid Sheikh Mohammed, the self confessed mastermind behind the Twin Towers atrocity, to be held in a Manhattan courtroom close to Ground Zero promises to revive the controversy, because defence lawyers may well draw attention to his being waterboarded a total of 183 times during his time at Guantanamo Bay.

Extraordinary Rendition (2006)

American security services have been accused of transporting terrorist suspects to regimes using harsher interrogation techniques than those allowed within the US.

Background

Terrorism is a horribly effective weapon, which can strike innocent victims without warning. Security organizations can only fight back by obtaining information on plans, intentions, and capabilities from suspects falling into their hands, who routinely deny having any such information or any part in terror organizations. Barred from using undue pressure on their prisoners to extract information, and charged with protecting the wider public, these conflicting requirements are almost impossible to fulfil. In an attempt to resolve this dilemma, the US Central Intelligence Agency (CIA) began flying suspects to overseas countries where they remain outside US legal safeguards or restrictions on torture. Since the term "rendition" was used to refer to routine flights taking people accused of a crime in an overseas country to face justice in that country, this much more secret and illegal version was given the description "extraordinary rendition."

Deception

During the mid-1980s, following a succession of terrorist acts, the US Congress passed laws declaring that air piracy (hijacking) and attacks on US citizens overseas were Federal crimes, and in 1986 President Reagan authorized the CIA to kidnap terrorist suspects anywhere in the world, to bring them to the US for trial. A year later, Fawaz Yunis, who had hijacked a Jordanian airliner with American passengers on board, was kidnapped on a

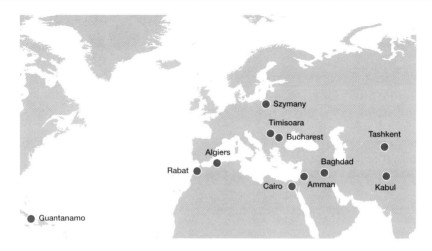

Above Map showing suspected transfer points where detainees were unlawfully transported between different countries.

boat in international waters off Cyprus and placed in American custody. In 1995, President Bill Clinton signed an authorization for the CIA to use rendition with suspects as part of a campaign to combat Al Qaeda's growing power in the Middle East. Since most of the suspects were Egyptian, the Egyptian Government was eager to have them back in its control, where they would be subject to severe interrogation and punishment. After the Twin Towers atrocity of September 11, 2001, the pace quickened, as the CIA came under severe criticism for failing to obtain inside information, which would have revealed what the terrorists had been planning. Soon afterward, NATO members agreed secretly to give blanket clearance to all covert military flights by allied aircraft engaged in operations against terrorism, which clearly covered extraordinary rendition.

Exposure

The truth about extraordinary rendition first appeared on December 4, 2005 in the *Washington Post*. It described suspects being masked, blindfolded, and sedated, and flown to countries collaborating in extraordinary rendition, or to "black sites," CIA prisons in remote places where officers could use the most robust interrogation techniques. National and international opinion reacted sharply: The US Senate moved to pass a law demanding regular updates on any secret detention facilities overseas, and details of the condition and treatment of every individual prisoner. The Council of Europe claimed in 2006 that 100 European Union (EU) citizens had been seized from European territory and flown to other countries under extraordinary rendition, often by way of black sites under CIA control. The European Parliament published a report in February 2007 claiming that, in direct contravention of European law on human rights and UN conventions, the CIA had carried out no fewer than 1,245 of these secret flights.

Fallout

Defenders of extraordinary rendition deny that torture is involved, but insist legal interrogation is a great deal more effective when carried out by people from the same culture and speaking the same language as suspects. When asked in a radio interview in April 2006 if rendition flights went to countries where torture is practiced then Secretary of State, Condoleeza Rice, specifically denied this was the case. However, the *Washington Post* was strongly criticized for not having revealed the precise locations of the "black sites," and the newly elected President Obama signed an Executive Order two days after his inauguration to outlaw extraordinary rendition as a means of subjecting terrorist suspects to torture, and to set up a task force to suggest how the practice could be prevented.

Glossary

Auditors: accountants employed to check and certify the accuracy of a company's accounts.

Bank rate: interest rate paid by banks to investors on the money they deposit.

Bills of exchange: documents issued and guaranteed by a bank which can be presented at another bank and credited to the recipient's account.

Bonds: documents issued by governments and institutions which pay good rates of interest in return for depositors leaving their money in place for a fixed minimum time.

Boosting share values: fraudulent means of increasing a company's assets through secret buying of its own shares on the open market, causing the value of those shares to rise without reflecting a genuine improvement in the company's financial position.

CBE: Commander of the British Empire, an honor first created during Lloyd George's Premiership in the 1920s, a higher-ranking version of the OBE.

Chapter 11 bankruptcy: US legal provision which allows a company facing bankruptcy to continue trading while efforts are made to reach an agreement with its creditors.

Class action: a form of lawsuit where a large group of people collectively bring a claim to court, which acts as a precedent for future claims on similar grounds.

Competitive tendering: a process where companies competing to win a contract have to submit individual tenders so that the most economical bid can be chosen, to avoid fraud and ensure optimum value for money.

Conflict of interest: a situation where lawyers or accountants, supposed to act as impartial monitors of a company's operations enjoy substantial benefits from doing what the company wants.

Inflating bills: fraudulently marking up the amount due on a bill; the fraudster pockets

Control rods: components in a nuclear reactor used to regulate the speed of the chain reaction. Because they are made from materials which can absorb neutrons without damage, inserting control rods into the reactor reduce the number of neutrons in the reaction, and slow it down—withdrawing the rods leaves more neutrons free to continue the reaction, which speeds up as a result.

Court of Cassation: the highest ranking court in the French judicial system.

Deregulation: removal of legal restrictions on the operation of a particular market, allowing many more companies to enter that market with less careful monitoring.

Electronic warfare: tactics involving gathering information on enemy radar, guidance and communication systems, or interfering with those systems to conceal one's own operations.

Freezing accounts: preventing the withdrawal of funds from the accounts of companies or individuals suspected of fraud or insolvency.

Holocaust survivors: members of Jewish families who had escaped being murdered by the Nazis during the Second World War, and who in many cases were seeking to retrieve family funds deposited in Swiss banks before and during the conflict.

Immunity from prosecution: a deal done to enable a person with inside knowledge of a fraud to trade providing vital evidence for escaping punishment for their own role in the fraud.

Impeachment: a legal process which can end in the dismissal of a US President for committing "high crimes and misdemeanours" while in office.

the difference when the bill is paid.

Inside knowledge: information on future market conditions unknown to the public which enables an individual or a company to make an unfair profit in share trading.

Limpet mine: a watertight charge which can be fixed to the hull of a ship below the waterline by a diver, with a timing device to blow a hole in the plating and sink the vessel.

Money laundering: complex financial transactions to conceal the criminal origins of profits from drugs, extortion, fraud, and other illegal activities.

OBE: Order of the British Empire, an honour first created under Lloyd George's Premiership in the 1920s.

Penny share trading: buying shares in fledgling companies at bargain prices in the hopes of future success and a steep climb in share values.

Pension fund: large sums amassed by companies to pay for future pensions for their employees on retirement, and a prime target for criminal directors needing cash.

Ponzi scheme: another term for pyramid selling, named after Carlo Ponzi, who ran the first of these frauds.

Proxy voting: a system whereby shareholders can vote on important issues affecting a company by filling in official forms to register their decision, without having to attend the shareholders' meeting in person.

Pyramid selling: an investment fraud where deposits from the original investors are used to suggest falsely high profits, and attract more and more participants.

Rendition: transporting extradited criminals to face justice in a country where they had committed crimes. "Extraordinary rendition" refers to clandestine flights to carry terrorist suspects to countries for interrogation under specially harsh conditions.

SEC: Securities and Exchange ommission—

US financial trading watchdog.

Second home allowances: money paid to British Members of Parliament to reimburse them for the costs of maintaining a second residence, either close to Westminster or in the constituency they represent.

Semaphore stations: a chain of signal stations linking the Admiralty in London with the principal ports, where the movements of a pair of arms could relay a message quickly along the entire line.

Short straddle: technical term for a market trade which effectively bets on the market staying relatively stable, when it can prove highly profitable. However, if the market rises or falls more sharply, losses can be equally large.

Skyspot: US radar-guided precision control system used to steer bombers to their targets and trigger the dropping of bombs on target, without the need for visual target finding.

Sub-contracting: a trading connection where a company under contract to a client employs a third company to supply it with necessary goods or services to enable it to fulfil its own contract.

Unsecured loans: loans issued without the borrower having to provide security against failure to repay the loan.

Vote manipulation: a fraud where the result of a shareholders' vote can be changed by adding extra names of people bribed to vote to the shareholder register.

Waterboarding: brutal interrogation technique which simulates the sensations of drowning to persuade suspects to reveal information.

WMD: weapons of mass destruction— nuclear, chemical, and biological weapons with the capability to cause enormous casualties if used by rogue states.

Sources

Internet

Time Magazine: *www.time.com*
New York Times: *www.nytimes.com*
Washington Post: *www.washingtonpost.com*
The Guardian: *www.guardian.co.uk*
The Times: *www.timesonline.co.uk*
Daily Telegraph: *www.telegraph.co.uk*
Financial Times: *www.ft.com*
US Security and Exchange Commission: *www.sec.gov*
Reuters: *www.reuters.com*
CBC: *www.cbc.ca*
BBC: *www.bbc.co.uk* and *news.bbc.co.uk*
The Australian: *www.theaustralian.news.com.au*
Risk Glossary website: *www.riskglossary.com*
About North Georgia: *www.ngeorgia.com/history*
The New Georgia Encyclopaedia: *www.georgiaencyclopedia.org*

Literature

Carswell, John, *The South Sea Bubble* (Sutton Publishing: Stroud, UK, 2002)
Balen, Malcolm, *The Short History of the South Sea Bubble—the World's First Great Financial Scandal* (Fourth Estate: London, 2003)

Bidwell, Austin, *From Wall Street to Newgate*, (True Crime Library: London, 1996)

Thomas, Donald, *Cochrane: Britannia's Sea Wolf*, (Cassell Military Paperbacks: London, 2001).
Dale, Richard, *Napoleon is Dead: Lord Cochrane and the great Stock Exchange Scandal*, (Sutton Publishing: Stroud, UK, 2006).

Index

Abu Ghraib prison 135
Air Canada scandal 63–64
Airbus Industries 63–64
Al Qaeda 133, 135, 137
Aquino, Benigno 85
Aquino, Corazon 85
Australian Wheat
    Board scandal 90–91

Banco Ambrosiano
    fraud 28–30
Bank of England fraud 19–20
banknotes, forged 26–27
Barings Bank collapse 60–62
Bell, Martin 109
Berlusconi, Silvio 112–14
Bernhard, Prince
    (of Netherlands) 53
Bidwell, George and
    Austin 19–20
Black, Conrad 65–66
Blix, Hans 130
Boeing 63
Boesky, Ivan 56–57
Bottomley, Horatio 24–25
Brandt, Willi 106–7

Calvi, Roberto 28–30
Cambodia, bombing
    of 128–29
Carter, President Jimmy 53
cash for honors
    scandal 98–99
cash for questions
    scandal 108–9

Chappaquiddick incident
    103–5

Chen Liangyu 67–68
Chernobyl disaster 86–87
China: pensions
    scandal 67–68
CIA 76, 133–35, 136–38
Clinton, President Bill
    110–11, 129, 137
Contra rebels 81–83
Cosmos fraud 54–55
Crédit Mobilier fraud 50–51

Denning inquiry 102
Diana Princess of Wales 109
Distillers group 56
Downey enquiry 109
Dreyfus affair 120–21

Ebbers, Bernard 58–59
Enron Corporation 36–38
extraordinary rendition 133,
    136–38

Fall, Albert B. 96–97
Fayed, Mohammed 108, 109
Ford, President Gerald 78
France: Dreyfus affair 120–21
    Société Général fraud
    69–71
FSB 92–93

George V, King 99
Germany: Brandt spy
    scandal 106–7
Greenpeace 79
Greer, Ian 108, 109
Gregory, Maundy 98–99
Guantanamo Bay 133, 135
The Guardian 108–9

Guinness fraud 56–57
Hamilton, Neil 108–9
Harding, President
    Warren G. 96–97
Harriman, Ned 17–18
Hezbollah 81
Hollinger International
    65–66
Holocaust bank accounts
    33–35
Hong Kong shares fraud
    72–73
honors, sale of 98–99
Hu Jintao, President 67–68

India: Satyam fraud 42–44
Iran-Contra scandal 81–83
Iraq 90–91, 130–32
Italy: Berlusconi scandals
    112–14

Jackson, Senator James 13–14
Japan: Bank of 31–32
    Recruit fraud 54–55
John Paul I, Pope 30
Johnson, President
    Lyndon/Johnson
    administration
    122–24, 129
Jones, Paula 110

Keeler, Christine 100–102
Kelly, Dr David 132
Kennedy, Senator Edward
    103–5
Kennedy, President John F.
    122
Kerviel, Jérôme 69–71

KGB 92, 93
Khmer Rouge 129
Kopechne, Mary Jo 103–5

Lay, Kenneth 38
Leeson, Nick 60–63
Lewinsky, Monica 110–11
Li, Richard 72–73
Litvinenko, Alexander 92–93
Lloyd George, David 98–99
Lockheed scandal 52–53
Lugovoi, Andrei 92, 93

Madoff, Bernard 39–41,
    45, 46
Major, John 108, 109
Marcinkus, Archbishop
    Paul 30
Marcos, Ferdinand 84–85
Maxwell, Robert 88–89
Mitterrand, President 80
MPs' expenses scandal
    115–17
Mulroney, Brian 63–64
My Lai massacre 125–27

Napoleon death fraud 15–16
New Zealand: *Rainbow
    Warrior* 79–80
Nicaragua 81–83
Nixon, President
    Richard/Nixon
    administration 76–78,
    127,128, 129
North, Colonel Oliver 81–83

Obama, President Barack
    105, 135, 138
Operation Menu 128–29
Oregon land fraud 17–18

P2 Masonic Lodge 29
Pacific Century CyberWorks
    (PCCW) 72–73
pension fund scandal 88–89
Philippines: Marcos regime
    84–85
Poindexter, John M. 83
Polonium 210 92-93
Ponzi, Carlo 21–23, 45, 46
Ponzi schemes 21–23,
    40–41, 46
Portuguese banknotes,
    forged 26–27
Profumo, John 100–102
Puter, Stephen A. Douglas
    17–18
pyramid selling
    see Ponzi schemes

Rainbow Warrior 79–80
Raju, B. Ramalinga 42–44
Reagan, President
    Ronald/Reagan
    administration
    81–83, 136
Recruit fraud 54–55
Reis, Arthur Virgilio 26–27
Roux, Olivier 57

Saddam Hussein 90–91,
    130–32
Sandinista government 81–82
Satyam Computer Services
    42–44
Saunders, Ernest 56–57
Sihanouk, Prince 128–29
Skilling, Jeffry 38
Smith, Tim 108–9
Société Général fraud 69–71
South Sea Bubble 10–12
Stanford, Sir Allen 45–47

Starr, Kenneth 111
Stasi secret police 107
Swiss banks and Holocaust
    accounts 33–35

Teapot Dome scandal 96–97
Thompson, Warrant Officer
    Hugh 126
Tonkin Gulf incident 122–24
torture, use of 133–35, 138
Twin Towers 133, 135, 137

Union Pacific Railroad 50–51

Vatican Bank fraud 28–30
Victory Bonds fraud 24–25
Vietnam War 122–23,
    125–27, 128–29

Walpole, Robert 12
Ward, Stephen 100–102
Washington Post 76–77,
    137, 138
Watergate 76–78, 81
weapons of mass destruction
    (WMD) 130–32
WorldCom fraud 58–59

Yazoo land fraud 13–14
Yoshizawa, Yasuzuki 31–32

Zola, Émile 121

This 2010 edition published by Metro Book,
by arrangement with Elwin Street Limited

Conceived and produced by
Elwin Street Limited
144 Liverpool Road
London N1 1LA
www.elwinstreet.com

Design and icon illustration: Jon Wainwright
All other illustrations: Richard Burgess

Picture credits:
Alamy: p. 89; Corbis: pp. 50, 102, 104, 124, 134;
Getty: pp. 29, 35, 43, 61, 62, 66, 70, 77, 80, 82, 101,
111, 113, 117, 126; Photolibrary: p. 11

Metro Books
122 Fifth Avenue
New York, NY 10011

ISBN: 978-1-4351-1774-7

Printed and bound in China

10 9 8 7 6 5 4 3 2 1